Insiders – Outsiders

edited and annotated
by
Liesel Hermes

Langenscheidt-Longman
ENGLISH LANGUAGE TEACHING

Viewfinder
Literature

Insiders - Outsiders

Herausgeber:
Peter Freese

Bearbeitung:
Liesel Hermes

Desktop-Publishing:
Bettina Lindenberg
Sabine Schalwig (Wißner Verlag)

Umwelthinweis: Gedruckt auf chlorfrei gebleichtem Papier

1. Auflage 1996

© 1996 Langenscheidt-Longman, München

Das Werk und seine Teile sind urheberrechtlich geschützt. Jede Verwertung in anderen als den gesetzlich zugelassenen Fällen bedarf deshalb der vorherigen schriftlichen Einwilligung des Verlages.

Druck: Schoder Druck GmbH & Co. KG, Gersthofen
Printed in Germany

ISBN 3-526-50 784-8

Contents

Introduction	4
Wendy Wallace	
Karif	7
Annotations	12
Tasks	14
Jane Gardam	
Swan	15
Annotations	28
Tasks	30
Elizabeth Raintree	
Sumac on a Sunday	32
Annotations	36
Tasks	37
Jane Stone	
The Man	39
Annotations	47
Tasks	48
Ron Butlin	
The German Boy	50
Annotations	54
Tasks	55

Introduction

The short stories in this collection are linked not by their origin or authorship but through their content. All of them deal - in a variety of ways - with "outsiders", individuals who find themselves in some way on the outside of a particular group or society in general.

How does it feel to be an outsider? I am sure, you and your class will have in various situations in your lives experienced what it means not to belong to a group or a majority, to be different, alone, to feel isolated. Before embarking on the stories, you should therefore have a brainstorming session and share your experiences in class of feeling or actually being an outsider in some special situation in your lives. You may wish to take into account situations such as
- being in a foreign country,
- living with a family you do not know,
- being in a class together with students of different nationalities,
- being the only one with certain political, ethical or religious convictions.

You may then like to discuss the thoughts and feelings or even anxieties that accompany the situation of an outsider.

How do "insiders" treat people they consider to be outsiders? They may either ignore or isolate them, they may actually humiliate, harass or discriminate against them, or they may on the other hand tolerate and accept them and try to include and integrate them into the "mainstream".

You will have realised that outsiders are always part of some minority, may it be social, ethnic or religious or of some other kind. People may come from a "foreign" country or simply look "strange" to us. In order to familiarise yourselves with the meanings of these two words, look them up in the *Longman Language Activator*. The descriptions and explanations listed may give you food for thought on how people deal verbally with human beings who are or seem to be different or behave in a way that seems unfamiliar to us. You may come to realise that the term "outsider" or "insider" is largely a subjective judgment and that depending on perspective, "outsiders" can also be "insiders" and vice versa!

Dealing with the short stories in *Insiders - Outsiders*, it seems important to establish who in each story actually is "inside" and who is "outside" and on what grounds we come to our conclusions. Next you may try to account for your reasons for assigning the characters in the stories an insider or outsider position. This has always to be seen in relation to the other characters in the story as well as to the setting. Last, it is of utmost importance to determine the narrative perspective. Is the story seen through the eyes of an "insider" or an "outsider"? You may find that empathy, i.e. the ability to feel with a character, last but not least depends on the narrative perspective chosen by the author. Therefore it may be a challenging task to rewrite the stories, changing the perspective from that of an "insider" to the "outsider". If you do that with at least one of the stories you will find that it opens up new ways of understanding the original text.

The present collection consists of five stories by authors who are not yet well-known. Each story is preceded by a short biographical note where details of the authors are known. In the case of Jane Stone, no further information is available but you may like to try to find out more yourselves.

There are multiple thematic links among the texts. In "Karif", the first-person narrator, a pregnant young English woman living in London, observes Rushna, a woman from Bangladesh and her three children, who live in the house next to hers. Although there are indications that the narrator tries to help Rushna, whose husband is in Bangladesh, the reader may wonder to the very end if she really makes an effort to empathise with Rushna and her children.

In "Swan", an English boy from a private school in London does some social work and takes care of a Chinese immigrant boy named Henry Wu and, over a period of about a year, tries to understand him and his Chinese background.

In "Sumac on a Sunday", a young woman, a Native American of the Cherokee tribe, who has been adopted by a white American couple, is at the centre of the action. In a flashback the reader learns about her childhood with the white family.

"The Man" deals with an old man who has come to live in a village in Yorkshire and has no contact whatsoever with its inhabitants except for a group of children who come to play in his garden.

"The German Boy" is by far the most complex story. The first-person narrator, a businessman expecting the bankruptcy of his firm, while watching a woman in the street, remembers a German boy who during World War II joined his class in an English school. The boy neither understood nor spoke English and remained isolated although the narrator tried to befriend him.

Literature can help you gain an insight into other cultures. Except for "The Man", all the other stories deal with several cultures and with the difficulties involved when someone lives in a foreign country and either resists its way of life and culture or tries to adapt to it and become integrated. "Karif", "Swan" and "The German Boy" take the insider's narrative perspective, "Sumac on a Sunday" the outsider's. The title character in "The Man" lives in total isolation, his only human contact being the children who are still free of prejudice.

Being an outsider can happen on the grounds of race, just as well as of age. In "Karif", Rushna's children find their own way of coping with their situation of living in England. In "Swan", Pratt tries to empathise with the Chinese family and Henry, just as the first-person narrator does in "The German Boy" with Klaus. In "Sumac on a Sunday" it is the outsider who tries to adapt to the white American culture.

The stories can be read either as a sequence or individually. The tasks should be understood as suggestions which may help you find your way into each individual text.

I would like to thank the students of my *Hauptseminar* at the University of Koblenz in the winter semester 1994/95 for their discussions on the texts and their helpful contributions and ideas. Many thanks are also due to Dr. Christian Klinnert (Bildungszentrum Pfinztal), who read the short stories and made valuable comments on their suitability for their use in the English classroom. I wish to thank Qaizra Shahraz of Manchester and the photographers of the Karlsruhe newspaper *Badische Neueste Nachrichten* for giving permission to publish the photos.

The book is for Claudia.

Koblenz, 1996

WENDY WALLACE

Wendy Wallace, born in 1956, is an English journalist and writer. Her interest in other cultures comes both from working in Africa in the 1980's and from living in Hackney, a multi-cultural area of London. Having written a novel (unpublished) and several short stories - two of which were published in Sleeping Rough, Lime Tree *(1991) - she now writes mainly for newspapers and magazines. She is married to a photographer, and they have two children.*

Karif

We moved into our houses in the spring. We were both interlopers, Rushna and I. Me with my car and my briefcase and her with her bright flowing clothes and private language. In this backwater of the capital, too far from anywhere to be called inner city, too unkempt and populous to count as suburban, we stood out.

In our different ways, we set about making our houses our own. I hung black and white photographs of other countries on the walls and put up Venetian blinds at the windows. She looped a curtain of beads over the inside of the front door and got a cherry red carpet which covered the living room floor and stretched down the hall and up the stairs. She laid it herself, cutting the edges with the dressmaking scissors in careful, frayed lines.

Our houses were identical but we lived in them differently. Her kitchen was bare, home only to a cooker, a fridge and a formica-topped table, lit from above by an unforgiving neon tube. She kept sacks of rice and onions under the sink and the rest of the food in the fridge, even the tins of baked beans which the children liked. They called them English food. She cooked twice a day with vegetables and spices and occasionally a chicken. She made large quantities and ate little herself, didn't even sit down at the table if one of her relatives came to visit. She wasted nothing. When the dustbinmen didn't come, her rubbish didn't rot and spill over the front path like mine did, but accumulated modestly in the bottom of the black plastic dustbin.

My kitchen looked frivolous and overcrowded compared with hers. My Spanish plates hung on one wall, strangers to food. The table was piled with newspapers and letters, thrown into relief in the evenings by the sideways light of the Anglepoise lamp. The smell of her cooking often drifted through the window to me as I opened a tin of soup or got a quiche out of the freezer. I cooked little and ate a lot. I was eating for two. I had a passion for hot things. On feast days she passed little delicacies over the fence. 'Oony', she would call, if she heard me in the garden. 'Moment'. Then her hand would appear over the top of the fence, holding a plateful of salty yellow doughnuts or lentil fritters flavoured with garlic and coriander.

For a long time I didn't notice that she too was pregnant. She already had three children. A baby of about one and two older children, a boy and girl. Her husband was away, in Bangladesh. She showed me a photograph of him, a small man standing in front of an Indian restaurant on the Holloway Road and looking into the distance with a strange smile on his face.

The weather was exceptionally good that year. If I looked down from the window of my workroom, where I sat with the hum of the word processor, I would see her working in the garden, her sari blowing in the breeze like a foreign flag. I was working on a book on urban children. I called it work, although I was making slow progress. In a couple of months, she transformed the bare patch of earth behind her house into a small farm with rows of onions, a great bed of lacy-leaved coriander and a thicket of runner beans which sprang up along the fence.

Some mornings she would have a friend in the garden with her, standing on the path talking while Rushna cut spinach leaves or dug potatoes. Her friend was older than Rushna; she was plain while Rushna was pretty, solid by comparison with Rushna's slightness. Perhaps she reminded Rushna of her mother, who she missed. She had showed me a photograph of her too, pulling the well-thumbed album out of the suitcase on top of the wardrobe in her bedroom. Some of the photographs in the album were torn in half, to remove the memory of people with whom she had quarrelled. She had no problems of cultural identity, Rushna. Bangladesh was her country and Bengali her language. She just happened to be living in England.

Late at night, when the voices of her children had finally quietened, I would hear the soft swish of falling rain in the next garden as she trod up the path watering her plants in the darkness.

My garden was for pleasure, I could see that when I looked down on it. I had a bird bath, and a wicker table not sturdy enough to support more than a bottle of wine. Alongside the bathroom wall a row of geraniums stood dying in their little pots. I couldn't find time, somehow, to water them. The pale roses in my garden rested their heads against the high wooden fence we had put up between the two gardens, so we would have our privacy. I sometimes regretted that fence. It kept the sun off Rushna's mustard plants, and leaned alarmingly when the wind blew.

By July, my baby was due. I was large and ungainly. Next to Rushna, I felt like a giant schoolgirl in my Mothercare dungarees in their conspicuously cheerful colours. I was older than her, and knew nothing of children. But once I had had my baby, I felt that we had motherhood in common, if not language. In the still of the night, in the hours before dawn, we could hear each other's babies crying through the thin brick walls which separated our bedrooms, while outside the electric milk float whirred in stops and starts along the silent street.

Her older children, Rumana and Rubel, soon became friends with my baby, Benjamin. They were tender and patient with him and I was grateful to them for it. They began coming to the house every day after school, bringing him a drawing they had done in class or a paper crown decorated with gold stars. They called me 'aunty', and so, when he was old enough to talk, did my son.

Rumana was ten and liked pretty clothes. She wore shiny turquoise pantaloons with crooked seams, run up on Rushna's machine. Some days she came with a red silk carnation in her hair and chipped pink varnish on her nails. She was an exotic little bird, in scuffed schoolgirl shoes and wrinkled socks, her only concessions to English clothes. Occasionally I would hear the two children arguing about whether their father was coming back. Rushna hadn't heard from him.

They were almost the only Asian children in their school, and it was hard for them. The teacher tried to make them feel at home, getting the class singing 'one chappatti, two chappattis, three chappattis four.' But they came home for lunch because they didn't like eating with knives and forks, didn't like fish fingers and thought hamburgers had ham in them. In the playground, the other girls laughed at Rumana's homemade clothes.

Rumana often had her baby sister balanced on her narrow hip. She was adept at looking after her, lugging her around to where the others were playing and bringing her little objects to amuse her. Rubel, her brother, took no responsibility for the baby. At eight, he had already adopted something of a swaggering posture. He shouted and farted and refused to go to Bengali school on Saturday morning. 'Because if I go there, then I'm gonna be Bengali, innit,' he reasoned. He had eczema on his face and arms and one night, when I called round to borrow some onions, he answered the door wearing woolly gloves.

Towards the end of the summer, Rushna was looking weary. She still worked in her garden occasionally, while the older children were at school. Sometimes she just stood stock still, gazing at her plants and resting one hand on top of her high, hard belly. Perhaps she felt the new baby twisting inside her. It didn't seem as if her husband would arrive in time to see him born. She still sent round gifts of food - lentil soup in a fluted, pearlised bowl or a few sticks of rhubarb wrapped in newspaper. More rarely, she came herself, with combed hair and round gold earrings, lowering herself carefully onto the couch and setting the toddler on the floor for a few minutes.

In the end, the baby was born at home. Rumana had called me, shouting through the letterbox that Rushna was getting her baby. I rang for an ambulance but by the time it arrived the baby had been born. Rushna made no fuss, no noise, just gave birth on the cherry red carpet in the hall while her friend paced the kitchen floor calling on God to save them. It was a boy.

Once the ambulance had taken them off to the hospital, her friend sprang into action, pulling the curtains and putting on the lights. She served the children with food from the pots sitting ready on the cooker and put the kettle on for tea. She pointed out a tiny stain on the carpet in the hall and began scrubbing at it with satisfaction. The children ate ravenously, in silence.

Rushna was discharged from the hospital with a letter for the midwives and a packet of condoms. She could not name her baby until she had spoken to her husband. The children called him 'little brother' and touched his shaved head affectionately. Now there were two baby's cradles standing by the double bed in Rushna's room, and two sets of cries coming through the wall at night, one a high, mewing sound.

Little brother's wizened face fleshed out and his liquid eyes began to focus. Rushna said her husband had telephoned. She said there was bad news at home, but she didn't say what. Every night on television they showed pictures of Bangladesh submerged under water and women stranded on rooftops holding babies who looked like little brother.

I was no longer sure that Rushna and I had motherhood in common. She was bringing up her family on less than I was paying Benjamin's childminder. She could only leave the house for a few minutes at a time, when both babies slept. She had no time for her garden, which took on a yellowing, disconsolate look. She sent round packets of instant mash with the children, instead of the fresh produce. Rumana didn't come to play so much any more. She stayed at home to help her mother with the babies. Sometimes she didn't even go to school

One Sunday, at Rushna's request, I took them in the car to visit some cousins. Rushna wore here wedding gold and lipstick. She looked beautiful. Rumana had on lipstick too, and beads on top of her frilly party dress. Rihana wore a green spotted dress with matching pants over her nappy and little brother lay awkwardly in a small printed shirt with its collar round his ears. Rubel wore his dark school trousers and kept his hands in his pockets.

The cousins were well-off. They had two display cabinets full of ornaments in the front room, and a video. Rushna and her cousin greeted each other in a perfunctory way and immediately began what sounded like an argument. After some time, the women sent the children out to play. We were going to watch a video, of a recent family wedding in Bangladesh.

The film began in the bride's bedroom, with the camera panning unsteadily around the faces of the numerous women in attendance. One was attaching a long black plait to the bride's hair, another painting intricate patterns on her face. The camera lingered on the blue silk-lined vanity case on the end of the bed, spilling over the cosmetics. It showed the faces of young girls, apparently bored, and older women, animated and shiny-eyed. Their voices were drowned on the tape by the jangling, insistent sound of Bangla music.

The bride herself was very young. Sixteen, Rushna's cousin said. She sat passively, eyes downcast, while she was prepared and discussed. Finally, the grandmother placed a red shawl over the girl's head and the bride was led from the room. The film continued with the bridegroom, standing in a grove of palm trees surrounded by his male friends. He wore a brilliant white frock coat and white trousers. He had garlands of flowers around his neck and on his head a golden turban. The camera zoomed in on his face, and I recognised the faraway smile of Rushna's husband.

Rushna's cousin froze the video, using the remote control, and we sat in silence on the velour couches. The children's voices floated into the room from outside and little brother began his high, hiccoughing cry. 'Bad news,' said Rushna, pulling her sari tighter around her. 'Bad news.' Then she called sharply to Rumana to bring her sister and we left.

The next day Rushna chose a name for her son. It was Karif, meaning born in the Autumn. She took him to the Town Hall and registered his birth, signing her name uncertainly in the blue record ink. She put the certificate away with the wedding gold and the condoms, alongside the photographs in the suitcase on top of the wardrobe. She never did tear the children's father out of her wedding photographs.

Annotations

1 **interloper** (n.): s.o. who enters a place or group where they should not be - 2 **briefcase** (n.): case used for carrying papers and documents - 3 **backwater** (n.): very quiet place not influenced by outside events - 4 **unkempt** (adj.): not neat or tidy - 8 **Venetian blind** (n.): set of long flat bars of plastic or metal which can be raised or lowered to cover a window - 8 **to loop** (v.): to fasten or join with a loop (Schlinge, Schlaufe) - 12 **frayed** (adj.): with loose threads at the edges - 14 **formica** (n.): (tdmk.) strong plastic made in thin sheets, used especially for covering the surfaces of tables - 16 **sink** (n.): open container in a kitchen that is filled with water for washing dishes etc - 23 **to accumulate** (v.): to gradually increase in amount - 23 **to throw into relief**: to make very different from everything else around and therefore easy to notice - 28 **Anglepoise lamp** (n.): (tdmk.) type of lamp that can be moved into different positions - 31 **feast** (n.): day when there is a religious festival - 35 **lentil** (n.): kind of vegetable (Linse) - 35 **fritter** (n.): thin piece of fruit or vegetable covered with a mixture of eggs and flour and cooked in hot fat - 35 **garlic** (n.): plant like a small onion, used in cooking to give a strong taste - 44 **word processor** (n.): small computer used especially for writing texts - 46 **urban** (adj.): connected with a town or city - 48-49 **lacy-leafed** (adj.): with leaves that look like lace - 49 **thicket** (n.): group of bushes and small trees - 54 **slightness** (n.): (here) thinness - 67 **wicker** (adj.): made from thin dry branches woven together - 67 **sturdy** (adj.): strong and well-made - 73 **mustard** (n.): Senf - 75 **ungainly** (adj.): moving in a way

that does not look graceful - 76 **Mothercare dungarees** (n.): (tdmk.) loose trousers that have a piece of cloth that covers your chest and long thin pieces that fasten over your shoulders - 77 **conspicuous** (adj.): easy to notice because it is different from everything else - 82 **milk float** (n.): vehicle used for delivering milk to people's houses - 82 **to whirr** (v.): to make a fairly quiet regular sound (e.g. regular movement of part of a machine) - 85 **tender** (adj.): gentle - 86 **grateful** (adj.): feeling that you want to thank s.o. - 91 **crooked** (adj.): /ˈkrʊkɪd/ not in a straight line - 91 **seam** (n.): line where two pieces of cloth have been sewn together - 92 **carnation** (n.): kind of flower (Nelke) - 92 **chipped** (adj.) - 93 **varnish** (n): liquid painted on your finger nails with small pieces broken off - 93 **scuffed** (adj.): shoes that are scuffed are marked from wearing - 94 **concession** (n.): s.th. that you allow s.o. - 99 **chappatti** (n.): kind of bread, small flat pancake eaten in India - 105 **adept** (adj.): good at doing s.th. - 105 **to lug** (v.): to pull or carry s.o. heavy with difficulty - 108 **to swagger** (v.): to walk proudly - 108 **posture** (n.): /ˈpɒstʃə/ position you hold your body in - 109 **to fart** (v.): (taboo) to make air come out of your bowels - 111 **eczema** (n.): /ˈeksɪmə/ condition in which your skin becomes dry, red and swollen - 116 **to gaze** (v.): to look at s.o. or s.th for a long time - 120 **fluted** (adj.): decorated with long narrow curves that curve inwards - 120 **pearlised** (adj.): with a pearl-like surface - 123 **toddler** (n.): very young child who is just learning to walk - 135 **ravenous** (adj.): extremely hungry - 137 **midwife** (n.): specially trained nurse whose job it is to help women when they are having a baby - 142 **to mew** (v.): /mjuː/ to make a soft high crying sound like a cat - 143 **wizened** (adj.): /ˈwɪzənd/ s.th. small and thin with a skin full of lines and wrinkles - 146 **submerged** (adj.): just under the surface of water - 153 **disconsolate** (adj.): /dɪsˈkɒnsələt/ feeling extremely sad and hopeless - 160 **frilly** (adj.): having many decorative folds of cloth - 161 **awkward** (adj.): /ˈɔːkwəd/ behaving in a way that does not look comfortable - 164 **display cabinet** (n.): piece of furniture with glass doors and shelves - 166 **perfunctory** (adj.): a perfunctory action is done quickly and only because people expect it - 170 **to pan** (v.): of a camera that moves and follows the thing that is being filmed - 171 **in attendance** (n.): at a special or important event - 173 **intricate** (adj.): /ˈɪntrɪkɒt/ containing many small parts or details - 173 **to linger** (v.): /ˈlɪŋgə/ to stay somewhere a little longer - 174 **vanity case** (n.): small bag used by a woman for carrying make-up etc. - 177 **to jangle** (v.): /ˈdʒæŋgəl/ if metal objects jangle they make a sharp sound when hit - 183 **frock coat** (n.): knee-length coat for men - 190 **to hiccough** (v.): /ˈhɪkʌp/ to make sudden uncontrolled quick movements of the diaphragm (Zwerchfell) (einen Schluckauf haben) - 196 **certificate** (n.): /–ˈ– –/ official document that states that a fact or facts are true

Tasks

1: Pre-reading: One of the two women in the story comes from Bangladesh. Collect all the information you can find about the country. Refer to an atlas and to reference works (e.g. *Fischers Weltalmanach*). Prepare a short talk about Bangladesh.

2: The two women can be contrasted and compared at the same time. Find out all points of comparison. Take into account their life-styles, kitchens, gardens, etc.

3: In line 1 the women are both called "interlopers". Find proof in the text that this term is justified, although with different connotations.

4: Rushna is said to have "no problems of cultural identity" (line 60). Find proof for this in the text.

5: Discuss Rushna's children's problems with their lives at home and outside respectively. What differences are there between the elder boy and the girl?

6: Rushna is discharged from hospital with a pair of condoms. What does this tell the reader about the woman's role, as envisaged by the hospital doctors and nurses?

7: How is tension created in the part of the story, when the women watch the video?

8: Evaluate Rushna's symbolical acts at the end of the story of giving her baby a name and of not cutting her husband out of her wedding photographs.

9: There is very little dialogue in the story. Everything is told in a matter-of-fact way. Discuss whether the story is therefore lacking in emotion.

10: Is there any evidence that the narrator tries to understand Rushna, her position and her situation?

11: What is your attitude to Rushna at the end of the story? Discuss your assessment with a partner.

JANE GARDAM

Jane Gardam was born in Coatham in North Yorkshire and studied at London University. Before turning to writing she worked as a Red Cross Travelling Librarian and as sub-editor for various magazines. Her novels include God on the Rocks *(1978), for which she won the Prix Baudelaire,* The Hollow Land *(1981), which won the Whitbread Literary Award, and* The Queen of the Tambourine *(1991), for which she received the Whitbread Novel Award. Her collection of short stories* The Pangs of Love *(1983) won the Katherine Mansfield award. Other collections are* Showing the Flag *(1989), from which "Swan" is taken, and* Going into a Dark House *(1994).*

Swan

Two boys walked over the bridge.

They were big boys from the private school on the rich side of the river. One afternoon each week they had to spend helping people. They helped old people with no one to love them and younger children who were finding school difficult. It was a rule.

'I find school difficult myself,' said Jackson. 'Exams for a start.'

'I have plenty of people at home who think no one loves them,' said Pratt. 'Two grandparents, two parents, one sister. '

'And all called Pratt, poor things,' said Jackson, and he and Pratt began to fight in a friendly way, bumping up against each other until Jackson fell against a lady with a shopping-trolley on a stick and all her cornflakes fell out and a packet of flour, which burst.

'I'm going straight to your school,' she said. 'I know that uniform. It's supposed to be a good school. I'm going to lay a complaint,' and she wagged her arms up and down at the elbows like a hen. Pratt, who often found words coming out of his moth without warning, said, 'Lay an egg. Cluck.'

'That's done it. That's finished it,' said the woman. 'I'm going right round now. *And* I'll say you were slopping down the York Road Battersea at two o'clock in the afternoon, three miles from where you ought to be.'

'We are doing our Social Work,' said Pratt. 'Helping people.'
'Helping people!' said the woman, pointing at the pavement.
'We're being interviewed to take care of unfortunate children,' said Jackson.

'They're unfortunate all right if all they can get is you.' And she steamed off, leaving the flour spread about like snow, and passers-by walked over it giving dark looks and taking ghostly footprints away into the distance. Pratt eased as much of it as he could into the gutter with his feet.

'She's right,' he said. 'I don't know much about unfortunate children. Or any children.'

'They may not let us when they see us,' said Jackson. 'Come on. We'd better turn up. They can look at us and form an opinion.'

'Whatever's that mess on your shoes?' asked the Head Teacher at the school on the rough side of the river, coming towards them across the hall. 'Dear me. It *is* a nasty day. How do you do? Your children are ready for you, I think. Maybe today you might like just to talk to them indoors and start taking them out next week?'

'Yes, please,' said Jackson.

'Taking them *out*?' said Pratt.

'Yes. The idea is that - with the parents' consent - you take them out and widen their lives. Most of them on this side of the river never go anywhere. It's a depressed area. Their lives are simply school (or truanting), television, bed and school, though we have children from every country in the world.'

'It's about the same for us,' said Pratt. 'Just cross out television and insert homework.'

'Oh, come now,' said the Head Teacher, 'you do lots of things. Over the river, there's the Zoo and all the museums and the Tower of London and all the lovely shops. All the good things happen over the bridge. Most of our children here have scarcely seen a blade of grass. Now - you are two very reliable boys, I gather?' (She looked a bit doubtful.) 'Just wipe your feet and follow me.'

She opened a door of a classroom, but there was silence inside and only one small Chinese boy looking closely into the side of a fish-tank.

'Oh dear. Whatever...? Oh, of course. They're all in the gym. This is Henry. Henry Wu. He doesn't do any team games. Or - anything, really. He is one of the children you are to try to help. Now which of you would like Henry? He's nearly seven.'

'I would,' said Pratt, wondering again why words kept emerging from his mouth.

'Good. I'll leave you here then. Your friend and I will go and find the other child. Come here, Henry, and meet - what's your name?'

'Pratt.'

'Pratt. HERE'S PRATT, HENRY. He's not deaf, Pratt. Or dumb. He's been tested. It is just that he won't speak or listen. He shuts himself away. PRATT, HENRY,' she said, and vanished with an ushering arm behind Jackson, closing the door.

Henry Wu watched the fish.

'Hello,' said Pratt after a while. 'Fish.'

He thought, that is a very silly remark. He made it again, 'Fish.'

The head of Henry Wu did not move. It was a small round head with thick hair, black and shiny as the feathers on the diving ducks in the park across the river.

Or it might have been the head of a doll. A very fragile Chinese-china doll. Pratt walked round it to try and get a look at the face, the front of which was creamy-coloured with a nose so small it hardly made a bump, and leaf-shaped eyes with no eyelashes. No, not leaf-shaped, pod-shaped, thought Pratt, and in each pod the blackest and most glossy berry which looked at the fish. The fish opened their mouths at the face in an anxious manner and waved their floaty tails about.

'What they telling you?' asked Pratt. 'Friends of yours, are they?'

Henry Wu said nothing.

'D'you want to go and see the diving ducks in our park?'

Henry Wu said nothing.

'Think about it,' said Pratt. 'Next week. It's a good offer.'

Henry Wu said nothing.

'Take it or leave it.'

Pratt wondered for a moment if the Chinese boy was real. Maybe he was a sort of waxwork. If you gave him a push maybe he'd just tip over and fall on the floor. 'Come on, Henry Wu,' he said. 'Let's hear what you think,' and he gave the boy's shoulder a little shove.

And he found himself lying on the floor with no memory of being put there. He was not hurt at all - just lying. And the Chinese boy was still sitting on his high stool looking at the fish.

Pandemonium was approaching along the passage and children of all kinds began to hurtle in. They all stopped in a huddle when they saw large Pratt spread out over the floor, and a teacher rushed forward. The Head Teacher and Jackson were there, too, at the back, and Jackson was looking surprised.

'Oh dear,' said the teacher, 'his mother taught him to fight in case he was bullied. She's a Black Belt in judo. She told us he was very good at it. Oh Henry - not again. This big boy wants to be kind to you.'

'All I said,' said Pratt, picking himself up, 'was that I'd take him to the diving ducks in the park. What's more, I shall,' he added, glaring at Henry Wu.

'Why bother?' said Jackson. They were on their way home. 'He looks a wimp. He looks a rat. I don't call him unfortunate. I call him unpleasant.'

'What was yours like?'

'Mine wasn't. She'd left. She was a fairground child. They're always moving on. The school seems a bit short of peculiar ones at the moment. I'll share Henry Wu the Great Kung Fu with you if you like. You're going to need a bit of protection by the look of it.'

But in the end Jackson didn't, for he was given an old lady's kitchen to paint and was soon spending his Wednesdays and all his free time in it, eating her cooking. Pratt set out the following week to the school alone and found Henry Wu waiting for him, muffled to just below the eyebrows in a fat grasshopper cocoon of bright red nylon padding.

'Come on,' said Pratt, and without looking to see if Henry followed, set out along the grim York Road to a bus stop. Henry climbed on the bus behind him and sat some distance away, glaring into space.

'One and a half to the park,' said Pratt, taking out a French grammar. They made an odd pair. Pratt put on dark glasses in case he met friends.

It was January. The park was cold and dead. The grass was thin and muddy and full of puddly places and nobody in the world could feel the better for seeing a blade of it. Plants were sticks. There were no birds yet about the trees, and the water in the lake and round the little island was heavy and dark and still, like forgotten soup.

The kiosk café was shut up. The metal tables and chairs of summer were stacked inside and the Coke machine was empty. Pigeons walked near the kiosk, round and round on the cracked tarmac. They were as dirty and colourless as everything else but Henry looked at them closely as they clustered round his feet. One bounced off the ground and landed on his head.

Henry did not laugh or cry out or jump, but stood.

'Hey, knock that off. It's filthy,' shouted Pratt. 'They're full of disease, London pigeons. Look at their knuckles - all bleeding and rotten.'

A large black-and-white magpie came strutting by and regarded Henry Wu with the pigeon on his head. The pigeon flew away. Henry Wu began to follow the magpie along the path.

'It's bad luck, one magpie,' said Pratt, 'One for sorrow, two for joy,' and at once a second magpie appeared, walking behind. The

Chinese boy walked in procession between the two magpies under the bare trees.

'Come on. It's time to go,' said Pratt, feeling jealous. The magpies flew away, and they went to catch the bus.

Every Wednesday of that cold winter term, Pratt took Henry Wu into the park, walking up and down with his French book or his Science book open before him while Henry watched the birds and said nothing.

'Has he *never* said anything?' he asked the Head Teacher. 'I suppose he talks Chinese at home?'

'No. He doesn't say a thing. There's someone keeping an eye on him of course. A Social Worker. But the parents don't seem to be unduly worried. His home is very Chinese, I believe. The doctors say that one day he should begin to speak, but maybe not for years. We have to be patient.'

'Has he had some bad experiences? Is he a Boat Person?'

'No. He is just private. He is a village boy from China. Do you want to meet his family? You ought to. They ought to meet you, too. It will be interesting for you. Meeting Chinese.'

'There are Chinese at our school.'

'Millionaires' so from Hong Kong. I expect, with English as their first language. This will be more exciting. These people have chosen to come and live in England. They are immigrants.'

'I'm going to meet some immigrants,' said Pratt to Jackson. 'D'you want to come?'

'No,' said Jackson to Pratt, 'I'm cleaning under Nellie's bed where she can't reach. And I'm teaching her to use a calculator.'

'Isn't she a bit to old for a calculator?'

'She likes it. Isn't it *em*igrants?'

'No, immigrants. Immigrants come *in* to a country.'

'Why isn't it innigrants then?'

'I don't know. Latin, I expect, if you look it up. Emigrants are people who go out of a country.'

'Well, haven't these Chinese come out of a country? As well as come in to a country? They're emigrants and immigrants. They don't know whether they're coming or going. Perhaps that's what's the matter with Henry Wu.'

'Henry's not an innigrant. He's a *ninny*grant. Or just plain *innigrant*. I'm sick of him if you want to know. It's a waste of time, my Social Work. At least you get some good food out of yours. You've started her cooking again. And you're teaching her about machines.'

'Your Chinese will know about machines. I shouldn't touch the food, though, if you go to them. It won't be like a Take-Away.'

'D'you want to come?'

'No thanks. See you.'

'Candlelight Mansions,' said the Social Worker. 'Here we are. Twelfth floor and the lifts won't be working. I hope you're fit.'

They climbed the concrete stairs. Rubbish lay about. People had scrawled ugly things on the walls. On every floor the lift had a board saying out of order hung across it with chains. Most of the chains were broken, too, so that the boards hung crooked. All was silent.

Then, as they walked more slowly up the final flights of stairs, the silence ceased. Sounds began to be threaded into it; thin, busy sounds that became more persistent as they turned at the twelfth landing and met a fluttery excited chorus. Across the narrow space were huge heaps. Bundles and crates and boxes were stacked high under tarpaulins with only the narrowest of alleys to lead up to the splintery front door of Henry Wu's flat. A second door of diamonds of metal was fastened across this. Nailed to the wall, on top of all the bundles, were two big makeshift birdcages like sideways chickenhouses and inside them dozens of birds - red and blue and green and yellow - making as much noise as a school playground.

'Oh dear,' said the Social Worker, 'here we go again. The Council got them all moved once but the Wus just put them back. They pretend they don't understand. Good afternoon, Mrs Wu.'

A beautiful, flat Chinese woman had come to the door and stood behind the metal diamonds. She did not look in the least like a Black Belt in judo. She was very thin and small and wore bedroom slippers, a satin dress and three cardigans. She bowed.

'I've just called for a chat and to bring you Henry's kind friend who is trying to help him.'

Mrs Wu took out a key and then clattered back the metal gate and smiled and bowed a great deal and you couldn't tell what she was thinking. From the flat behind her there arose the most terrible noise of wailing, screeching and whirring, and Pratt thought that Jackson had been right about machines. A smell wafted out, too. A sweetish, dryish, spicy smell which sent a long thrill down Pratt's spine. It smelled of far, far away.

'You have a great many belongings out here,' said the Social Worker, climbing over a great many more as they made their way down the passage into the living-room. In the living-room were more again, and an enormous Chinese family wearing many layers of clothes and sitting sewing among electric fires. Two electric sewing-machines whizzed and a tape of Chinese music plinked and wailed, full-tilt. Another, different tape wailed back through the open kitchen door where an old lady was gazing into steaming pans on a stove. There were several birdcages hanging from hooks, a fish-tank by the window and a rat-like object looking out from a bundle of hay in a cage. It had one eye half-shut as if it had a headache. Henry Wu was regarding this rat.

The rest of the family all fell silent, rose to their feet and bowed. 'Hello, Henry,' said Pratt, but Henry did not look round, even when his mother turned her sweet face on him and sang out a tremendous Chinese torrent.

Tea came in glasses. Pratt sat and drank his as the Social Worker talked to Mrs Wu and the other ladies, and a small fat Chinese gentleman, making little silk buttons without even having to watch his hands, watched Pratt. After a time he shouted something and a girl came carrying a plate. On the plate were small grey eggs with a skin on them. She held them out to Pratt.

'Hwile,' said the Chinese gentleman, his needle stitching like Magic. 'Kwile.'

'Oh yes,' said Pratt. (Whale?)

'Eat. Eat.'

'I'm not very...'

But the Social Worker glared. 'Quail,' she said.

'Eggs don't agree...' said Pratt. (Aren't quails snakes?) He imagined a tiny young snake curled inside each egg. I'd rather die, he thought, and saw that for the first time Henry Wu was looking at him from his corner. So was the rat.

So were the fish, the birds, Mrs Wu, the fat gentleman and all the assorted aunts. He ate the egg which went down glup, like an oval leather pill. Everyone smiled and nodded and the plate was offered again.

He ate another egg and thought, two snakes. They'll breed. I will die. He took a great swig of tea and smiled faintly. Everyone in the room then, except the rat, the fish and Henry, began to laugh and twitter and talk. The old woman slipper-sloppered in from the kitchen bringing more things to eat in dolls' bowls. They were filled with little chippy things and spicy, hot, juicy bits. She pushed them at Pratt. 'Go on,' said the Social Worker. 'Live dangerously.'

Pratt ate. Slowly at first. It was delicious. 'It's not a bit like the Take-Away,' he said, eating faster. This made the Chinese laugh. 'Take-Away, Take-Away,' they said. 'Sweet-and-Sour,' said Mrs Wu. 'Not like Sweet-and-Sour,' and everyone made tut-tutting noises which meant, 'I should just hope not.' Mrs Wu then gave Pratt a good-luck charm made of brass and nodded at him as if she admired him.

'She's thanking you for taking Henry out,' said the Social Worker as they went down all the stairs again.

'She probably thinks I'm a lunatic,' said Pratt, 'taking Henry out. Much good it's done.'

'You don't know yet.'

'Well, he's not exactly talking, is he? Or doing anything. He's probably loopy. She probably thinks I'm loopy, too.'

'She wouldn't let you look after him if she thought you were loopy.'

'Maybe she wants rid of him. She's hoping I'll kidnap him. I'm not looking after him any more if he can't get up and say hello. Or even smile. After all those terrible afternoons. Well, I've got exams next term. I've got no time. I'll have to think of myself all day and every day from now on, thank goodness.'

And the next term it was so. Pratt gave never a thought to Henry Wu except sometimes when the birds began to be seen about the school gardens again and to swoop under the eaves of the chapel. Swallows, he thought, immigrants. And he remembered him when his parents took him out to a Chinese restaurant on his birthday.

'Oh no - not those,' he said.

'They are the greatest Chinese treat you can have,' said his father. 'Quails' eggs.'

'Aren't they serpents?'

'Serpents? Don't you learn *any* general knowledge at that school? They're birds' eggs. Have some Sweet-and-Sour.'

'The Chinese don't have Sweet-and-Sour. It was made up for the tourists.'

'Really? Where did you hear that?'

'My Social Work.'

The exams came and went as exams do and Pratt felt light-headed and light-hearted. He came out of the last one with Jackson and said, 'Whee - let's go and look at the river.'

'I feel great. Do you?' he said.

Jackson said he felt terrible. He'd failed everything. He'd spent too much time spring-cleaning old Nellie. He knew he had.

'I expect I've failed, too,' said Pratt, but he felt he hadn't. The exams had been easy. He felt very comfortable and pleased with himself and watched the oily river sidle by, this way and that way, slopping up against the arches of the bridge, splashy from the barges. 'What shall we do?' he asked Jackson. 'Shall we go on the river?'

'I'd better go over and see if old Nellie's in,' said Jackson. 'I promised. Sorry. You go.'

Pratt stood for a while and the old lady with the shopping-trolley went by. 'Lolling about,' she said.

'I'm very sorry about your flour,' said Pratt. Filled with happiness because the exams were over he felt he ought to be nice to the woman.

But she hurried on. Pratt watched her crossing the bridge and found his feet following. He made for Candlelight Mansions.

'Does Henry want to come to the park?' he asked a little girl who peered through the diamonds. Her face was like a white violet and her fringe was flimsy as a paintbrush. There was a kerfuffle behind her and Mrs Wu came forward to usher him inside.

If I go in it'll be quails' eggs and hours of bowing, thought Pratt. 'I'll wait here,' he said firmly. Mrs Wu disappeared and after a time Henry was produced, again muffled to the nose in the scarlet padding.

'It's pretty warm out,' said Pratt, but Mrs Wu only nodded and smiled.

In the park Pratt felt lost without a book and Henry marched wordlessly, as far ahead as possible. The ice-cream kiosk was open now and people were sitting on the metal chairs. Pigeons clustered round them in flustery clouds.

'Horrible,' said Pratt, catching up with Henry. 'Rats with wings. I'll get you a Coke but we'll drink it over there by the grass - hey! Where are you going?'

Henry, not stopping for the pigeons, was away to the slope of green grass that led down to the water. On the grass and all over the water was a multitude of birds and all the ducks of the park, living ducks and pelicans and geese and dabchicks and water-hens and mallards. Old ducks remembering and new little ducks being shown the summer for the first time. Some of the new ducks were so new they were still covered with fluff - white fluff, fawn fluff, yellow fluff and even black fluff, like decorations on a hat. The proud parent ducks had large Vs of water rippling out behind them and small Vs rippled behind all the following babies. Henry Wu stood still.

Then round the island on the lake there came a huge, drifting meringue.

It was followed by another, but this one had a long neck sweeping up from it with a proud head on the end and a brilliant orange beak and two black nostrils, the shape of Henry Wu's eyes.

The first meringue swelled and fluffed itself and a tall neck and wonderful head emerged from that one, too.

Suddenly Henry pointed a short padded arm at these amazing things and, keeping it stiff, turned his face up to Pratt and looked at him very intently.

'Swan,' said Pratt. 'They're swans. They're all right, aren't they? Hey - but don't do that. They're not so all right that you ought to go near them.'

'Get that boy back,' shouted a man. 'They'll knock him down. They're fierce, them two.'

'Nasty things, swans,' said someone else.

But Henry was off, over the little green hooped fence, running at the swans as they stepped out of the water on their black macintosh feet and started up the slope towards him. They lowered their necks and started to hiss. They opened their great wings.

'Oh, help,' said Pratt.

'It's all right,' said the man. 'I'm the Warden. I'll get him. Skin him alive, too, if they don't do it first,' and he ran down the slope.

But the swans did not skin Henry Wu alive. As he ran right up to them they stopped. They turned their heads away as if they were thinking. They shifted from one big black leathery foot to another and stopped hissing. Then they opened their wings wider still and dropped them gently and carefully back in place. They had a purple band around each left leg. One said 888. White swans, purple band, orange beaks, red Henry Wu, all on the green grass with the water and the willows about them, all sparkling and swaying.

'Bless him - isn't that nice now?' said the crowd, as the Warden of the swans gathered up Henry and brought him back under his arm.

'You'll get eaten one day,' said the Warden, 'you'll go getting yourself harmed,' but he seemed less angry than he might.

On the way home Henry did not look at Pratt but sat with him on the long seat just inside the bus. It was a seat for three people and Henry sat as far away as possible. But it was the same seat.

Then Pratt went on his summer holidays and when he came back the exam results were out and they were not marvellous. He stuffed miserably about in the house. When Jackson called - Jackson had done rather well - he said that he was busy, which he wasn't.

But he made himself busy the next term, stodging glumly along, and took the exams all over again.

'Aren't you going to see your Chinese Demon any more?' asked Jackson afterwards. 'Come and meet old Nellie.'

'No thanks.'

'She says to bring you.'

'No thanks.'

But when the results came out this time, they were very good. He had more than passed.

Pratt said, 'How's Nellie?'

'Oh, fine. Much better tempered.'
'Was she bad tempered? You never said.'
'How's Henry Wu? Did you ever get him talking?'
'No. He was loopy.'

But it was a fine frosty day and the sun for the moment was shining and Pratt went to the park and over the grass to the lakeside where one of the swans came sliding around the island and padded about on the slope, marking time and looking at him.

It dazzled. The band round its leg said 887. 'Where's your husband?' said Pratt. 'Or wife or whatever? Are you hungry or something?'

The sun went in and the bare trees rattled. The swan looked a bit lonely and he thought he might go and get it some bread. Instead he took a bus back over the bridge and went to Candlelight Mansions.

They've probably forgotten me, he thought as he rang the bell. The bundles and the birdcages had gone from the landing. He rattled the steel mesh. They've probably moved, he thought. They'll have gone back to China.

But he was welcomed like a son.

'Can I take Henry out?'

Bowings, grinnings, buttonings-up of Henry who had not grown one millimetre.

'Where's the rat?' Pratt asked.

'Nwee-sance,' said Mrs Wu.

'Neeoo-sance,' said the fat gentleman. 'Nee-oosance. Council told them go.'

But the flat was now a jungle of floating paper kites and plants with scarlet dragons flying about in them, mixed with Father Christmases, Baby Jesuses and strings of Christmas tinsel. In the kitchen the old lady stirred the pots to a radio playing *O Come, All Ye Faithful*. Henry, seeing everyone talking together, sat down under a sewing-machine.

'Has he said anything yet?' asked Pratt, eating juicy bits with chopsticks. Everyone watched the juicy bits falling off the chopsticks and laughed. Now and then, when anything reached his mouth successfully, they congratulated him. They ignored the question, which meant that Henry had not.

It was cold in the street and very cold as they stood at the bus stop. Pratt had forgotten that the days were now so short, and already it was beginning to get dark. Far too late to go to the park, he thought. The bus was cold, too, and dirty, and all the people looked as if they'd like to be warm at home in bed. 'Come on - we'll go upstairs and sit in the front,' said Pratt and they looked down on the dreary York Road with all its little half-alive shops and, now and then, a string of coloured Christmas lights across it with most of the bulbs broken or missing. Some shops had spray-snowflakes squirted on the windows. It looked like cleaning fluid someone had forgotten to wash off. Real snowflakes were beginning to fall and looked even dingier than the shop-window ones.

I should have taken him over the river to see some real Christmas lights in Regent Street, thought Pratt. There's nothing over here.

But there came a bang.

A sort of rushing, blustering, flapping before the eyes.

The glass in the window in front of them rattled like an earthquake and something fell down in front of the bus.

There were screeching brakes and shouting people and Pratt and Henry were flung forward on the floor.

As they picked themselves up they saw people running into the road below. 'Something fell out of the sky,' said Pratt to Henry Wu. 'Something big. Like a person. Come on - we've got to get out.'

But it was not a person. It was a swan that sat heavy and large and streaked with a dark mark across its trailing wings in the very middle of the road.

'Swan, swan - it's a swan!' Everybody was shouting. 'It's killed itself. It's dead. Frozen dead with fright.'

'It hit a wire,' said someone else - it was the woman with the shopping trolley - 'I saw it. An overhead wire from the lights. They oughtn't to be allowed. They're not worth it. They could have electrocuted that bus.'

'It's killed it, anyway,' said Jackson, who seemed to be with her. 'It's stone dead.'

But the swan was not dead. Suddenly it decided it was not. It heaved up its head and wings and lolloped itself to the side of the road and flopped down again, looking round slowly, with stunned wonder, opening and shutting its orange beak, though with never a sound.

'It was migrating,' said the man from a chipshop.

'Swans don't migrate, they stay put, ' said a man from a laundry.

'Anyone'd migrate this weather,' said a man selling whelks and eels. 'Look, it's got a number on it. It's from the park. Look, it's put itself all tidy on the yellow line.'

'Out of the way,' said a policeman. 'Now then. Stand aside. We'll want a basket.' A laundry basket was brought and someone lent the policeman a strong pair of gloves.

'Clear a space,' he said and approached the swan, which proved it was not dead by landing the policeman a thwacking blow with its wing.

'Have to be shot,' said a dismal man from a bike-shop. 'Well, it's no chicken.'

'Course it's no chicken,' said the woman with the trolley. 'If it was a chicken it'd be coming home with me and a bag of chips.'

And then a girl with purple hair began to shriek and scream because she didn't believe in eating animals, which included birds.

'Anyway, all swans belong to the Queen,' said the trolley-lady. 'I heard it on Gardeners' Question Time.'

'I'm going crazy,' said the policeman, who had withdrawn to a little distance to talk into his radio-set. 'If they all belong to the Queen I hope she'll come and collect this one. I'm not sure I can. Move along now. We have to keep the traffic moving. We can't hold up London for a swan.'

One or two cars sidled by, but otherwise nobody moved. It was a strange thing. In the middle of the dead dark day and the dead dark street sat the open laundry basket and the shining, mute bird with its angel feathers. The road fell quiet.

Then Henry Wu stepped forward, small inside his padding, and put short arms round the bulk of the swan's back and lifted it lightly into the basket where it fluffed up its feathers like rising bread and gazed round proudly at the people.

'Heaven on high!' said everyone. 'The weight!'

'His mother's a Black Belt,' said Pratt proudly.

'That Chinese'll have to be washed,' said the trolley-lady. 'They'd better both come home with us, Jackson, and I'll give them their tea.'

But Pratt and Henry did not go home with old Nellie on that occasion because the policeman asked them to go back to the station with him and the swan. If Henry would be so kind as to assist him, he said. And Henry stroked the swan's docile head twice and then folded it down with its neck behind it - and a big strong neck it was, though very arrangeable - and quickly put down the lid.

The Park Warden came to the police station and he and Henry and Pratt and the swan then went on to the park, where the swan took to the water like a whirlwind and faded into the dark.

'Off you go, 888,' said the Warden. 'There's your missus to meet you. You wouldn't have seen her again if you'd not dropped among friends.

'They can't take off, you see,' he said to the two boys, 'except on water. They're like the old sea-planes.'

Pratt watched the two white shapes fade with the day. 'They're strange altogether, swans,' said the Warden. 'Quite silent!'

'Is is true they sing when they're dying?' asked Pratt. 'I read it. In poetry.'

'Well, that one's not dying then,' said the Warden. 'Gone without a sound. It's funny - most living creatures make some sort of noise to show they're happy. Goodbye, Henry. There'll be a job for you with creatures one day. I dare say when you grow up you'll get my job. You have the touch.'

On the bus back over the bridge to Candlelight Mansions Henry sat down next to Pratt on a double seat and, staring in front of him, said in a high, clear, Chinese-English voice, 'Hwan.'

'Hwan,' he said. 'Hwan, hwan, hwan, swan. Swan, swan, SWAN,' until Pratt had to say, 'Shut up, Henry, or they'll think you're loopy.'

Annotations

19 **to slop** (v.): (here) to move lazily - 20 **BATTERSEA:** an area and former borough of southwest London - 24 **unfortunate** (adj.): (fml). s.o. who has no money, home, job etc. - 29 **to ease** (v.): to move s.th. slowly and carefully into another place - 35 **mess** (n.): (here) dirt - 42 **consent**

(n.): permission to do s.th. - 44 **depressed** (adj.): here: with too little economic or business activity - 45 **to truant** (v.): (to play truant) to stay away from school without permission - 48 **to insert** (v.): put s.th. into s.th. else - 62 **to emerge** (v.): to appear or come out from somewhere - 67 **deaf** (adj.): physically unable to hear anything - 67 **dumb** (adj.): /dʌm/ physically unable to speak - 69 **to vanish** (v.): to disappear suddenly - 77 **fragile** (adj.): not strong and therefore easily broken - 81 **pod** (n.): long narrow seed container that grows on various plants, e.g. peas and beans - 95 **shove** (n.): strong push - 99 **pandemonium** (n.): situation in which there is a lot of noise because people are angry etc. - 100 **to hurtle** (v.): to move at a great or dangerous speed - 105 **to bully** (v.): to threaten or hurt s.o. especially s.o. smaller - 105 **BLACK BELT** (n.): a high rank in some types of Eastern self-defence, especially Judo and Karate - 112 **wimp** (n.): (infml.) s.o. who has a weak character or is afraid to do s.th. difficult or unpleasant - 115 **fairground child** (n.): a child that moves with his/her parents from one fair to another and never stays long in one place (??) - 116 **peculiar** (adj.): strange - 117 **KUNG FU** (n.): Chinese style of fighting without weapons that includes hitting with the hands and feet - 123 **padding** (n.): soft material used to fill or cover s.th. to make it warmer - 130 **puddly** (adj.): places full of small pools of water - 136 **tarmac** (n.): mixture of tar (Teer) and small stones, used for making the surface of roads - 137 **to cluster** (v.): to form a small group in a small place - 141 **filthy** (adj.): extremely dirty - 142 **disease** (n.): /dɪˈziːz/ illness - 144 **magpie** (n.): kind of black and white bird (Elster) - 151 **jealous** (adj.): feeling angry or unhappy because s.o. has s.th. that you would like - 161 **unduly** ((adv.): (fml.) too extreme or too much - 164 **BOAT PERSON** (n.): s.o. who escapes from conditions in their home country in small boats, hoping to find safety in other countries - 186 *ninny*****grant** (n.). (humour) ninny: silly person, here: play on words, cf. "innigrant" - 191 **TAKE-AWAY** (n.): shop that sells meals to be eaten somewhere else - 196 **concrete** (n.): substance used for building that is made by mixing sand, very small stones, cement, and water - 199 **crooked** (adj.): /ˈkrʊkɪd/ bent, twisted - 201 **to cease** (v.): /-s/ to stop - 202 **persistent** (adj.). continuing to happen - 204 **crate** (n.): box made of wood or plastic used for carrying fruit, bottles etc. - 205 **tarpaulin** (n.): /tɑːˈpɔːlɪn/ heavy cloth prepared so that water will not pass through it - 206 **diamonds of metal:** door made of metal bars (Drahtgitter) - 208 **makeshift** (adj.): made for temporary use - 214 **COUNCIL** (n.): organization that is responsible for local government in a particular region in Britain - 217 **cardigan** (n.): (infml.) knitted jacket - 223 **to whirr** (v.): to make a fairly quiet, regular sound - 224 **to waft** (v.): to move gently through the air - 225 **thrill** (n.): sudden strong feeling of excitement or pleasure - 225 **spine** (n.): row of bones down the centre of your back that supports your body - 240 **tremendous** (adj.): very powerful - 241 **torrent** (n.): (here) a lot of criticism that s.o. suddenly receives - 253 **quail** (n.): kind of bird (Wachtel) - 259 **assorted** (adj.): of various different kinds - 267 **spicy** (adj.): food that is spicy has a pleasantly strong taste - 271 **Sweet-and-Sour** (n.): in Chinese cooking, food that has both sweet and sour tastes together - 274 **charm** (n.): very small object worn on a chain that people think will bring them good luck - 274 **brass** (n.): yellow metal (Messing) - 277 **lunatic** (n.): /'– – –/ s.o. who behaves in a crazy or very stupid way - 281 **loopy** (adj.): (infml.) crazy or strange - 290 **eaves** (n. pl): the edges of a roof that stick out beyond the walls - 312 **arch** (n.): structure with a curved top and straight sides that supports the weight of a bridge - 312 **barge** (n.): low flat-bottomed boat - 323 **to peer** (v.): to look very carefully or hard - 324 **fringe** (n.): part of your hair that hangs over your forehead - 324 **kerfuffle** (n.): noise - 342 **dabchick** (n.): kind of water bird (Steißfuß oder Lappentaucher) - 343 **mallard** (n.): kind of wild duck - 350 **meringue** (n.): /məˈræŋ/ light sweet food made by baking a mixture of sugar and the white part of eggs - 363 **fierce** (adj.): (here) strong and wild - 366 **macintosh** (n.): /-k-/ coat worn to keep out the rain - 370 **warden** (n.): an official whose job it is to make sure that rules are obeyed - 379 **to sway** (v.): to move slowly from one side to another - 391 **to stodge** (v.): to walk with short heavy steps - 391 **glum** (adj.): sad and not talking much - 417 **mesh** (n.). a pice of material made of wires woven together like a net - 424 **nweesance = nuisance** (n.): /ˈnjuːsəns/ person, thing, or situation that annoys you - 429 **tinsel** (n.): thin strings of shiny paper used as decorations - 430 *O Come, All Ye Faithful*: Christmas song - 449 **dingy** (adj.): /ˈdɪndʒi/ dirty and dull or dark in colour - 451 **REGENT STREET**: street in the West End of London and popular for shopping - 467 **wire** (n.): thin metal in the form of a thread - 477 **to migrate** (v.): if birds migrate, they move from one part of the world to another - 479 **whelk** (n.): sea animal in a shell (Wellhornschnecke) - 480 **eel** (n.): long thin fish (Aal) - 488 **dismal** (adj.): /-z-/ unhappy and hopeless - 496 **to withdraw** (v.): to leave a place - 503 **mute** (adj.): not speaking - 506 **bulk** (n.): the main or largest part of s.th. - 516 **docile** (adj.): /ˈdəʊsaɪl/ quiet and easily controlled

Tasks

1: Pre-reading: The two English schoolboys in "Swan" do social work, e.g. they work for elderly people or take care of immigrants' children. What do you and your class think of such an idea?

2: Brainstorming: Collect information about swans. What kind of birds are they? Prepare a short talk. After finishing the story, discuss if the swans have a symbolical meaning.

3: Brainstorming: Discuss what a "depressed area" (line 44) may look like, how people live there and why such an area is called "depressed".

4: Time in this story covers about a whole year. Analyse the time structure and pay special attention to the alternation of scene and summary and their functions.

5: Characterise Henry Wu. Find instances for his special relationship with animals and try to account for it. Delineate the slow development he undergoes. What may be the reason that he does not speak at all until the very end?

6: Analyse Jackson's and Pratt's talk about "immigrants" (line 171). What linguistic problems emerge? Try to show how they reflect the Wu family's situation.

7: Investigate Pratt's visit to the Chinese family, together with the Social Worker. Take into account the surroundings, social circumstances, living conditions, and habits of the family. What do you think is Pratt's most important experience, and why?

8: Compare Pratt's experience with Chinese food at the Wus' with the one in the Chinese restaurant with his parents. Think of your own experiences with foreign food.

9: Comment on Pratt's relationship with Henry. Why does Pratt go on seeing Henry although he is "sick of him" (line 187) at times?

10: Examine the final scene with Swan 888. Describe the individual people's reaction to the swan and contrast it with Henry's.

11: Discuss Pratt's attitude to Henry and the development he has undergone. Pay special attention to the very last paragraph.

ELIZABETH RAINTREE

Elizabeth Raintree is an American writer who lives in London. She is an award-winning poet and has had fiction both published and broadcast. She has also published academic and political articles.

Sumac on a Sunday

Sumac was in her small apartment, lying on her bed. She had been lying there for quite a while. She was getting ready to do something hard. It got harder and harder, and took longer and longer each time.

She was preparing herself by lying still on her bed and visiting Randall's Woods to watch the birds. She could feel the Spring air in the Woods, sharp against the skin of her neck and shoulders. She could smell the earth thawing. On the unopened leaf buds of the old sycamores, she saw the first tinge of green. She walked, taking in the feel of the ground underfoot. Birds were everywhere. Sparrows and doves were already nesting.

Just then, church bells began to peal. Sumac remembered that it was Sunday, the appointed day, and found herself back in her bed in the attic of the big white frame house on Colony Street. She got up and went into the kitchen.

The rest of this day was planned. She would write home. That would take all day. And when it was done, she would not do anything else, because she would be too tired to do anything else.

Sumac filled the kettle, made herself a mug of strong black coffee, and carried it back into her one main room. Her unmade bed caught her eye and she made it neatly, pulling up the white bedspread her mother had given her three years ago. That was when she had left home to come to work in the big library here in the city.

Sumac settled herself with the coffee at the rickety desk and assembled letter paper and an envelope. Then she fished in the wastepaper basket for scrap paper. She always wrote her letters home first on scrap paper, until she felt sure she had all the words right.

She wrote, 'Dearest and Most Perfect Mother'.

A clock somewhere struck the hour and Sumac picked up her coffee. Somehow, she had lost some time. Perhaps a half hour. The coffee was stone cold. She drank it anyway because it was something she always did when she was about to write home. Then she realized that she had left out the most important parts of her writing-home ritual. She must fix her face, and she must cover her hair, completely.

Her parents had, after all, taught her proper ways. There was the bisque foundation. Then the ivory powder. Carefully, Sumac applied them. Together, they made her red-brown skin almost white.

Her hair presented a different sort of problem. She had been taught how to bob and bend and bleach it. But since she had come to the city, she had somehow fallen into the habits of not getting it cut, not setting it, and not even bleaching it. It was, consequently, after three years' neglect, exactly the straight black mane she knew she deserved. But her parents did not deserve to be in any way connected with it. That was why, before she wrote home, she always covered it. She had a large scarf which she took out of her bureau now and wrapped around her head so that not one strand of hair showed. Now she felt better. She was not Sumac. She was Sue. Her parents had named her Susan when they had adopted her. It was official. Her birth certificate said she had been born to Mr and Mrs Smith and that her name was Susan Smith.

Not that her parents had ever lied to Sumac about the facts. She knew that she was a Cherokee and that her biological mother - that was how Mrs Smith always put it - had been persuaded by conscientious social workers to give Sumac to their adoption agency for that reason. Mrs Smith had begun to teach Sumac's history to her almost before Sumac could understand the words. This was so that if she ever heard the truth from a neighbour in a moment of tactless candour, or from a neighbour child in a moment of childish spitefulness, Sumac would not come to her parents and accuse them of letting her believe herself falsely to be their real daughter.

It was all quite simple and straightforward, when the story was told the way Mrs Smith always told it. She and Mr Smith wanted a little girl of their own to love. They had one, but it died soon after birth. So they waited - actually, they left it rather long - in case Mrs Smith should produce a second baby. But as at forty-one, she still had not, they went to the agency. It turned out that Mr and Mrs Smith were too old to get a white baby, but the agency said they could have an Indian one. Mrs Smith accepted the situation graciously. She told Sumac that some of the best babies were Indian ones. And when her friends admired her for raising someone else's Indian baby as her own, she always replied smartly that it was not admirable at all - she had taken on the child to fulfil her own deep maternal needs.

Mr Smith was older by several years that Mrs Smith. Mr Smith always did admire *his* generosity, for he had allowed her to adopt Sumac and thus fulfil these needs. She explained to Sumac, who did not see much of Mr Smith, that he was very busy with his work. It made him very tired. That was why Sumac had to be bathed and fed her supper and put to bed before Mr Smith got home from work. Fathers, Mrs Smith told Sumac, loved their children very much. They showed it by working hard to provide for them, and coming home tired.

When Sumac was about five, Mrs Smith kept her up one evening just long enough to greet Mr Smith as a proper daughter should when he got home tired from work. Fed and freshly washed and dressed in her night-clothes, Sumac was led into the living room. 'Now kiss Daddy goodnight,' Mrs Smith said. Sumac went to the side of Mr Smith's big chair where he was sitting behind his newspaper. He did not seem to notice her, and Sumac looked at Mrs Smith to see whether this was all right. Mrs Smith nodded. Sumac held her breath and gave Mr Smith a little peck on the cheek.

Mr Smith told Mrs Smith on the spot that he wanted peace and quiet and his dinner. Mrs Smith told Sumac to go to bed. Then she served Mr Smith the dinner she had cooked for him.

'He loves you very much,' she reported to Sumac the next morning.

Soon after that, Mr Smith brought a bird trap. And a few days later, Sumac saw him entering the downstairs powder room with a live cowbird that he had caught. He was gripping the bird with one hand and opening the door with the other. He did not see Sumac. She heard the bird begin to screech and came to stand just outside the powder room door.

There was a strange, ominous, excited sound in Mr Smith's voice as he talked to the bird. 'Ah, my beauty,' Sumac heard him say.

She was about to knock on the door when she thought better of it, and kept on listening instead.

'You aren't going to like this very much, Sweetheart, but it's where you belong. Right in the toilet. Head, down, that's nice, under the water.'

The bird shrieked and there were splashing sounds.

'It's what you deserve. Laying your eggs in other birds' nests. That's what you do. Don't you?'

There was more splashing.

'And the good birds come home and find your eggs there, in their nest. And think they must be their own eggs. And hatch your babies for you. While their own eggs get pushed right out of the nest and never hatch at all. Well, you'll never do that again.'

Sumac could not move. She tried to see where her voice was and could not find it.

Mr Smith's voice became husky and almost tender. 'Don't worry, darlin',' he said. 'It doesn't last forever. We're almost there now, you and I.'

'Daddy!' screamed Sumac. Except that only a very small sound came out of her mouth.

Mr Smith heard it. 'You can't come in just now,' he called out to her through the door. 'I'm busy.'

The bird stopped squawking and the splashing ceased. Sumac did not wait for Mr Smith to come out of the powder room. She turned and ran upstairs to her room. As she was on her way, she heard Mr Smith saying to himself, 'They upset Nature. Better off dead.'

She watched him out of her window as he carried the limp bird out of the back door to the garbage can. He raised the can's lid and tossed the bird in.

Mrs Smith did not seem surprised to hear that Mr Smith had drowned a cowbird. 'They're not very nice,' she told Sumac. She added, 'Daddy likes to protect us womenfolk from wild creatures. Come, Susie. If you stop crying, I'll make you an ice-cream soda, with ginger ale and strawberry ice cream.'

Sumac didn't want anything to eat just then, but she did not want to be alone either, so she stayed in the kitchen with Mrs Smith and when the ice-cream soda appeared, she ate it because she could not think of any polite way not to.

Mr Smith became known in the neighbourhood, because of the size and elaborateness of his birdtrap, as a serious amateur naturalist with a specialization in ornithology, and people came to him on weekends with questions about the various kinds of birds they had seen in their own yards. He and Mrs Smith bought a set of bird books and joined the local bird club. They made friends there, including birdbanders and suppliers of birdseed as well as other birdwatchers like themselves.

Every morning when she first got out of bed, Sumac would kneel down in front of her open window and look out, and look at all the birds flying around, or perched on the big tree in the yard, or feeding at the birdfeeder that Mr Smith had hung outside her window, and she would just breathe, and try to understand birdness. She knew that was something which was not discussed at all in the bird books or at the bird club meetings. Birds were like guides, or lights, in a way. They ate Mr Smith's birdseed, but they were free, alive and complete in themselves, on their own out in the Universe. They were like Spirits. To watch them was like prayer.

Sumac knew this so deeply that nothing could shake it out of her. But finally she realized that she would never be able to explain it to Mrs Smith. One morning Sumac gave it one last try. Mrs Smith listened patiently. Then she said in a cheerful tone, 'Your very first word was "bird", dear. I taught you to say it. You were only six months old. I held you up and showed you the red bird ornament on top of our Christmas tree.'

The pen had slipped from Sumac's fingers and rolled over the edge of the desk onto the floor while she had been thinking how to begin her letter. She picked the pen up.

'Thank you,' she wrote slowly on the piece of scrap paper which so far said only, 'Dearest and Most Perfect Mother.'

'Thank you for the beautiful silky nightgown and the lacy panties.'

She pictured how Mrs Smith would read the letter to Mr Smith. Sumac was his daughter too, and it was his money that would have paid for the gift.

She crossed out 'nightgown' and 'lacy panties' and wrote 'lingerie'.

Annotations

7 **to thaw** (v.): if ice or snow thaws, it becomes warmer and turns into water - 7 **bud** (n.): young tightly rolled up leaf before it opens - 8 **sycamore** (n.) /ˈsɪkəmɔː/ kind of tree (Platane) - 8 **tinge** (n.): small amount of colour - 13 **frame house** (n.): house with a wooden frame covered with boards - 13 **attic** (n.): room under the roof of a house - 20 **neat** (adj.): tidy and carefully arranged - 23 **rickety** (adj.): /ˈ---/ a rickety piece of furniture looks as if it will break if you use it - 25 **scrap paper** (n.): paper that has already been used on one side, used for making notes etc. - 35 **bisque foundation** (n.): thick cream the same colour as your skin that you put on your face before the rest of the make-up - 35 **ivory** (n.): yellowish white colour - 38 **to bob** (v.): to cut s.o.'s hair so that it is the same length round the head - 38 **to bleach** (v.): to make s.th. white, especially by using chemicals - 40 **to set** (v.): (here) to arrange s.o.'s hair - 41 **mane** (n.): (infml.) a person's long thick hair - 44 **bureau** (n.): (in AE) /ˈbjʊroʊ/ piece of furniture with several drawers, used to keep clothes in - 51 **CHEROKEE** (n.): member of a Native American people from the US states of North Carolina and Tennessee - 53 **conscientious** (adj.): /kɒnʃiˈenʃəs/ showing a lot of care and attention - 57 **candour** (n.): truthfulness - 67 **gracious** (adj.): behaving in a polite and kind way - 95 **powder room** (n.): (in AE euph.) small room with toilet and washbasin - 96 **cowbird** (n.): small American blackbird that associates with cattle and lays its eggs in the nests of other birds - 100 **ominous** (adj.): /ˈ---/ making you feel that s.th. bad is going to happen - 111 **to hatch** (v.): a bird sits on eggs and hatches them until the young birds come out - 117 **husky** (adj.): deep and rough-sounding - 124 **to cease** (v.): to stop - 128 **limp** (adj.): not firm or strong - 129 **garbage can** (n.): (in AE) container with a lid for holding waste - 141 **elaborateness** (n.): /-ˈ----/ (here) trap with a large number of different or complicated parts - 142 **ornithology** (n.): scientific study of birds - 146 **birdbander** (n.): s.o. who puts bands round bird' legs - 170 **lacy** (adj.): made of or looking like lace (Spitze) - 170 **panties** (n.pl.): woman's underwear that covers the areas between her waist and the top of her legs - 174 **lingerie** (n.): /ˈlænʒəri/ women's underwear

Tasks

1: Pre-reading: Collect all the information you can find about Native Americans in general and the Cherokee tribe in particular. Consult your English textbooks and works of reference.

2: Pre-reading: A lot of babies or small children - also from abroad - are adopted by German parents every year. Discuss the pros and cons of adoptions (try to consider the children and the parents).

3: Establish the narrative perspective in this story and discuss its function.

4: Analyse the structure of the story. Pay special attention to the treatment of time and its function.

5: Collect all the details about Sumac's "parents" and family life. Examine the structure of the family, especially the wife's and husband's roles.

6: Discuss Mr. Smith's act of drowning the cowbird and his justification for the action. What may be the underlying motive for his behaviour?

7: Explain what may be meant by the sentences: "[The birds] were like Spirits. To watch them was like prayer." (lines 156-7)

8: The story if full of symbolism. Discuss the symbolical significance of the "white frame house" (line 13), "Colony Street" (line 13), the birds, Sumac's clothes, etc.

9: Discuss the ending: What may be Sumac's reason for changing the wording of her letter?

10: After-reading: You may want to read the short story "Raspberry Jam" by Angus Wilson, which also contains a scene in which two old women slowly kill a bird and the effect of this action on a small boy. Compare the two stories from this aspect.

JANE STONE

This story was discovered in British Short Stories of Today *(ed. Esmore Jones, Penguin Books, 1987). The author is otherwise unknown.*

The Man

No one knew when he came to the village. All that the adults, those proud possessors of worldly knowledge, could tell us was, 'He came.' One night, it was late September, and the house stood empty, as it always had, and we went up scrumping apples as we always had - well, no one claimed them now. The leaves were wet and soggy underfoot, and we frightened ourselves with tales of ghosts evolving out of the thin spirals of mist which wrapped around the trees.

That was the last time we ever climbed the apple tree, or watched the squirrels scurrying through the leaves to bed. The last time, that is, in play. The next night, the gate was locked, fences repaired, and lighted windows fended off even Johnny McCrae, who lost much status in consequence. But by far the most important thing was the old man who stood peering out of the curtainless windows downstairs. He wasn't very tall - he was stocky - he had a bushy moustache, thinning hair and he wore 'sort of baggy pants,' said Andy. 'Like a clown,' described Mary-Lou, but 'plus fours', corrected the grown-ups. 'Country gentleman's wear,' they added reverently - but we thought it a stupid name, for 'Plus means add,' said Andy. 'And four what?' he said.

For days after that we asked ourselves, 'Who is he?', bitterly resenting the interloper who had taken over our playground at such short notice. Until, one day, 'We gotta find out,' stated Andy. And when Andy stated anything, we did it.

That night the seven of us met, scared stiff, at the gates of the house. It was late now, and a solitary light flickered above the door. It came from the only room with curtains - at least at the front of the house. It was dark, and silent, and 'Let's go back, then,' whimpered Angie McClean, who always was a coward and never improved. 'Let's go *on!*' we said, in chorus.

Up the silent path, my heart jerking the strings of my cotton pinafore; up the path and across the strip of lawn we went. No one spoke because no one wanted to. That is a way with children. The stillness pressed upon us from behind, driving us up, up, into the relative sanctity of the long dark windows. Andy, longing to show off his knowledge of house-breaking, was as eager as a young bloodhound. It was common knowledge that Andy's brother had been the best clickie in the West Riding and it was also common knowledge that Andy showed promise far beyond his years. But as it happened that promise wasn't to be displayed. The door was open.

Andy's brother had not outrun his uses, however. From his pocket Andy produced a huge torch, with a beam so powerful that it illuminated the whole of the room we entered. It was a lovely room, long and high and spacious but, 'Heck!' said a disappointed Andy, 'It's empty.' And so it was. No carpets, no chairs; no heavy ugly dressers, concave mirrors, plaster dogs and plastic flowers such as made up the comfortable familiarity of our own homes. More sad than all these; the room was clean. Gleamingly, spotlessly clean. Our spirits fell, but, 'We might as well go on,' said Jo - so we crossed the room.

The door didn't creak as we opened it, like doors in mystery stories or the *Ghostly Tales* book I'd just been reading. No, this door was smooth, varnished, well-oiled. The hall into which it led was, surprisingly, circular, with a floor patterned in tiles of ivory and gold. In the centre stood a type of plinth - 'for a statue,' whispered Jo - but the statue must have gone visiting, and the hall was clean and bare.

We crossed the hall, forgetting for an instant to be silent, pulling up short, poised, ready to fly, as our serviceable steel-tipped shoes made contact with the tiles. 'Hope this'n's locked,' said Andy, darting towards the door. 'Wunna be,' stated Johnny. 'There inna nothin' worth takin'.'

He was right. It wasn't locked. And neither were any of the other doors. And not a single stick of furniture, thread of carpet or speck of dust did we see in any of them. The kitchen was of most interest, with a sink and a stove but, 'No food,' I said, in disappointment. I always was the greedy one.

So there we stood, a depressed little group, bunched at the foot of the stairs, debating whether to go on or back. Andy had just set his foot upon the bottom stair and Jo had turned towards the door when Angie McClean was sick. We looked at her in horror and we turned and ran.

Yet the next day, our appetite for the mystery was keener than ever. We organized a watching day to observe the movements which could be seen so clearly through the uncovered windows. There were six of us, so we split into twos and took shifts; Johnny and Mary-Lou for the morning, Andy and Jo for the afternoon, and Jimmy and me for the evening. Angie McClean, since her lapse of the previous day, was banned from our company.

By the end of the day we knew most of the man's movements. He rose late in the morning - by our standards at least, for we were mainly farmworkers' children and used to being up with the milk. Johnny and Mary-Lou, crouching in the orchard, watched a front window flung wide open, and there he was, short, stocky, 'in black pyjamas!' stated Johnny importantly, 'Black pyjamas, an' then he -' 'What?' we shouted in exasperation. 'He sorta jumped an' waved his arms about an' then' - his voice dropped to a whisper - 'he takes his clothes off, an' jumps about with nothin' on!' 'He does *not* then,' broke in Mary-Lou sharply, 'You can never tell anythin' straight Johnny McCrae. He had his trousers on.'

Then the man disappeared for a while, presumably for food, though where he had it we did not know. It occurred to us, though, that the upstairs rooms might possibly be more homely than those downstairs. Mary-Lou and Johnny had filled in the time by exploring the outhouses and found: 'Wood,' said Johnny, 'little tiny bits of wood, all done up in bundles.' 'And cloth,' broke in Mary-Lou excitedly, 'little packs of silk and stuff - all laid out on a table.' We wondered if he could be a carpenter, or a tailor, but 'there wasn't enough of anything,' said Johnny. 'Not to make things.'

After the exploration, they had picked up a few large apples, and sat in the shrubbery, munching and waiting. Some time later, the man came out through the front door and took a turn round the grounds. He walked carelessly over the damp garden, his heavy boots plodding aimlessly over rotting apples, brilliant michaelmas daisies and fallen rotten leaves. He stood for a while peering up at the gnarled apple trees, loaded with fruit. Then he went inside and with it. Hearing this hurt us most of all, for we had become so used to regarding the apples as our own particular property; it hurt us to think of their beautiful ripe redness as they tumbled higgledy-piggledy upon the grass. It hurt us to hear how the old man had gathered them up in a huge basket, taking them who knew where; perhaps to that high-up room of his. The damsons, too, were picked - 'the pig,' Mary-Lou had said, her mouth open and watering; 'he can't possibly want them all.'

He had come out on to the terrace afterward, with a pipe and a glass of beer, and sat, legs stretched out in front of him, alternately sipping and puffing, squinting at the tossing trees through the smoke. Then he disappeared again. Johnny and Mary-Lou watched and waited, as minute after minute went by, to try to get some inkling of what was going on. At length, they grew quite bold, leaving their hiding place in the shrubbery and going right round the house to see if they could see into the upstairs rooms. But there was no sign of movement, and when Andy and Jo came to relieve them, they shook their heads in disappointment.

Andy and Jo hid themselves in the orchard for the afternoon watch. 'He has his food upstairs, out of tins,' said Andy; and this wasn't all guesswork, for he was a good sleuth, and had spent some time educating himself with the contents of the dustbin, 'Sardines, baked beans, and - Spagg Hetty,' said Andy. None of us had heard of spaghetti before.

'And after his food?' we asked - if it *was* after his food - 'but I think it must be,' said Jo, 'because he sleeps.' 'Outside,' put in Andy; 'Even though it clouded over he still sat outside.'

Then came the operation that we knew must happen sometime - the time we'd been waiting for. 'A man, dusting and polishing,' scowled Andy, in disgust. 'An' why not?' said Jo. 'He's not got a woman.' 'But me *Dad* wouldna do it,' said Andy, as if that set the seal on things.

Jimmy and I came on duty just after tea. Ours was the dullest time of the day. We watched the light come on in the mysterious upstairs room, the only room with curtains. And all we could see were shadows. Shadows flickering here and there over the blinds; now a hand, now an arm, now some strange stump-like object waved about like a witch's wand. Crouching there in the damp leaves, with the mist just beginning to rise, we felt ourselves hard done by. 'Nothing happenin',' grumbled Jimmy. 'We gotta explore them rooms.' 'But not alone,' I said. I did not want him to think me a coward so, 'it wouldn't be fair to the others,' I said. Jimmy gave in, and we spent the rest of the evening munching sweets and windfalls, huddling together for warmth in the clammy mist, speculating about the strange ritual in the upstairs room. 'He probably murders rich women,' fancied Jimmy, 'cuts their clothes up and makes them into new cloth and then dries their bones to make wood.' I imagined my own bones joining that little pile of sticks and felt sick. 'I must know,' I said. 'Right,' said Jimmy, 'tomorrow night!'

By the next night we were tired of uncertainty, and walked boldly up to the windows, and into the room; we wasted no time there and went straight through the hall, though I noticed as we entered it that it was now clean and shining again.

We climbed the curved wooden staircase and found ourselves on a narrow landing with five doors opening off it; two one side, two the other, and one straight ahead - 'The Room,' whispered Andy. We stood for a moment and heard the sound of heavy breathing from a far door. 'He's in there,' said Jo: 'Come on.'

Silently we approached the end door. The door swung open, and Andy's torch flung the room into daylight.

We were spellbound. We even forgot to close the door in our awe. For the room was lined with deep, broad shelves, about eight to every wall. And from each shelf, regarding us unblinkingly, almost insolently, rows, and rows of '*dolls*?' said Andy, hesitantly, and his hesitation was not surprising, because 'They look ALIVE,' we breathed. Blue eyes, black eyes, brown eyes, smiling, staring, frowning, sulky, incurious, shining, sad, eyes flashing at us from faces that looked as if they should be soft and warm but, 'they *are* dolls,' said Johnny, as he poked one with his finger-tip.

There were sailor dolls, soldier dolls, beautiful girl dolls, bride dolls, fairy dolls, and best of all, foreign dolls. Dolls from almost every country in the world: sultry velvet-eyed maidens from the East, dark-haired vivacious señoritas from Spain, and prim little Dutch girls in clogs. I longed to cuddle the little fat Eskimo who smiled at me, it seemed, with fellow feeling. All were so exquisitely dressed that I couldn't see how anyone, least of all a man, could do such work.

'D'you think they move?' asked Josie at length, after our eyes had explored the long room. She stretched out her hand and took up a ballerina doll. It was fixed to a round wooden base, and behind it there was a key; Jo grabbed it and began to turn.

The ballerina doll had been poised on both toes, her arms reaching up above her head. Now, as Jo turned the key, the arms began to move, a little jerkily, swaying gently to a tiny, silvery tune. 'Like a musical box,' Andy told us. 'It's the music from Swan Lake,' breathed Mary-Lou, who went to weekly ballet class.

So enthralled were we by this spectacle that we forgot the open door. We forgot that we were in someone else's house, with that someone sleeping only one door away. We forgot to whisper, and forgot our steel-tipped shoes. And so we were terrified by the roar which suddenly came from behind us.

We turned, cowering, and met the man face to face. He was smaller than we thought, and stockier. His eyes were small, too, and now they glittered, deep blue and cold and clear, like blue sky over snow. His black pyjamas were no longer a cause for laughter - now they seemed horrific. We stood - he stood - and between us the little ballerina dropped to one knee as the last silvery strains of her music faded away.

He stood there, and his face was set in hate. He almost spoke, and then seemed to change his mind. He turned and strode out, slamming the door behind him. We half expected a key to turn, but it did not.

Yet we made no move to escape. By some kind of tacit general consent we all sat down on the floor. 'If it'd been me Dad,' said Jimmy uneasily, 'he'd have walloped us.' We nodded, for the thought was in all our minds. It bewildered us to be left thus, with no retribution: not even a long cussing which, by experience, we had all grown to expect from irate adults.

'He'll be waitin' for us downstairs,' said Johnny. But somehow we felt he wouldn't, and we felt guilty and uneasy. 'But we haven't *done* anything,' persisted Mary-Lou, 'only looked.' 'That's not it,' I said; 'they wasn't ours to see.'

'C'mon,' said Jimmy, standing up, 'we gotta say sorry.'

I shouldn't think any of us had ever said sorry to a grown-up in our lives - at least, not in a voluntary way. It just wasn't done. You had you walloping, and you moped for a while, and then everything went on as usual. Or else in really serious matters you were locked in your room until hunger forced an embarrassed kind of apology. But this was different. We stood up in a body and went to seek the man.

He was in his room we knew, for we could hear him moving about. Jimmy knocked on the door. After a while it opened a little and, 'I thought you'd've gone,' said the voice - surprisingly mild.

'We came to say...' Jimmy's voice trailed off. It was more difficult than he expected. 'Sorry,' almost shouted Mary-Lou, helping him out. 'Sir,' she added, remembering her manners.

The door jerked open suddenly: and he was smiling! He was smiling all over, and the black pyjamas were eclipsed by a bright red dressing gown. 'Well,' he said; 'that's the most difficult part of all. Come in.'

It was one of the oddest, yet pleasantest hours of my life. We were right about his food, because he produced a huge loaf from a cupboard filled with tins and he lit a gas ring in the corner of the room. We made huge piles of hot toast and loaded it with butter; and we made cocoa with evaporated milk that tasted like cream. For a while we were all too busy eating to talk, and his appetite, we noticed with satisfaction, was as keen as ours; we were too well used to the delicacy of grown-ups, who stopped after two sandwiches or one piece of cake and made you feel a pig if you asked for more.

So it wasn't until we slowed down a bit and started on chocolate biscuits and a large slab cake, that he asked us, 'What made you come?'

We looked at each other, and then Jimmy began to speak. He usually did the talking. He told him everything; about the garden, the apples, the watching, and the room. He told him how we had loved the dolls, and at the end he asked, 'Why d'you keep 'em all locked up, sir? Why don't you let people see 'em?' The old man extracted a large cherry from his piece of cake. 'It's a long story,' he said. 'And I'm not going to bore you with it.' I opened my mouth to say we wouldn't be - but closed it again on a warning look from Andy.

'Once,' said the man, 'I was married. Like most people. And like most people, I was happy. My wife was never strong, and three weeks before she had our baby she was ill. She died when out daughter was born.'

He spoke sadly, but without embarrassment, and so we felt no embarrassment either. This was odd, because in our homes, if anyone discussed birth, it was in a hushed voice, and with lowered eyes, which made us feel hot all over, and sometimes we were sent right out of the room.

'But you had your little girl?' I said - and then wished I hadn't, the man looked so sad.

'I had my little girl,' he said. 'But she couldn't walk or talk. She sat. Just sat.'

We said nothing.

'But don't think I didn't love her,' he said forcefully. 'She was my wife all over again. I made her dolls. She watched me while I made them, and I knew she knew I loved her and was making them for her - and I knew she loved them, so I made more and more. And when she died,' we sat unblinking, for we had been prepared for this; 'And when she died, before she died, she stretched out for her dolls, and over the dolls her eyes looked at me - so gratefully. I swore I'd go on making them. But they're *hers*, you see. No one else must see them. They're for her.'

'And then we came and saw them.' It was Jimmy again.

'Ah, well.' The old man stood up and he suddenly looked tired, 'You're children, after all. And what are dolls for, if not for children? I did not make them for myself. They were for her.'

Quietly he opened the door.

It was a signal for us to go; and we obeyed it. We shuffled out, and, turning, Jimmy had the last word.

'I'm sorry we upset you, sir - but I'm glad we come.'

We never went there again. Sometimes we thought of the lovely overgrown garden - but the jungle-like shrubberies, the broken branches we collected for Guy Fawkes' night, the climbable gnarled old trees - and as the blossom lent its fragile whiteness to the apple orchard we thought with regret of these rich red apples that autumn would bring. Sometimes, in the clear, sweet mornings of spring, we would think of the dolls, shut away in their curtained room: blank little eyes that never saw the sunlight, or the garden, or the springtime flowering of the shrubberies. And sometimes, we thought of the old man himself, and even thought he might like to see us again; but we hadn't been asked, and (with the quicksilver minds of children) we always had something else to do. In fact, now we knew the secret, we scarcely dwelt upon it; we were too practical to weave fantasies about it, too sensible to invite the scepticism and ridicule of the whole child population of the neighbourhood by telling our friends a story which they, and we, too, if it had been told to us, would have met with cries of 'The old cissy!' or 'Don't be so wet', or 'Give over, will yer, can't yer see I'm crying?'

So we dismissed the house, the man, the grounds, and life went on much as before. The long hazy summer days deepened again to autumn, and the corn began to be gathered from round about. The apples began to form upon the trees; acorns and bright polished conkers littered the ground. We collected blackberries glowing in the hedgerows, and wild hips and haws.

And then we noticed something strange about the old house. It was Johnny who first put it into words. 'Them apples is coming down,' he said. It was so, and the brilliant redness grew and grew upon the ground and still they were not gathered. The harsh bittersweet smell of rotting fruit began to grow, and now and then another would drop to its fellow with a splash. 'D'you think he's O. K.?' inquired Johnny at length.

We bore it uneasily for a few more weeks, but it was when the damsons began to fall that I said to Jimmy, 'We'll have to tell someone.' So, unwillingly, we told my mother, who shook her head and told us to run away and play.

It was two days later they buried him, and no one went to his funeral. We knew, because we tried to go, but the vicar and the sexton chased us off without listening to our explanations. Later, I hear my mother talking. 'Yes,' she said, 'they found him dead in bed. Awful old man - don't know what he did with himself. Some kind of hermit, most like - no, nothing in the house. All empty. So they just took him and came away.'

'And no one knows who he was?' queried my father.

'No. No family at all, s'far as they can make out. No job - like I said - it's not as if he *did* anything.' To my parents, this was the deadliest sin of all.

I turned away. I longed to burst in and tell her - 'you're stupid, you are, you're blind! Didn't you look in the little room - the one with a lock? Didn't you *see* them? The dolls, the dolls - the beautiful dolls?'

And then I remembered him saying, 'They were *hers*, you see. They were *hers*.' And I imagined what might happen to those dolls and I felt they might be better after all, up there, alone. And most of all, I knew what my mother would say if I tried to tell her what we saw.

So I picked up my coat and ran out into the autumn rain. And who knew that it wasn't the rain that damped my cheeks.

Annotations

4 **to scrump** (v.): (old-fashioned) to steal fruit, esp. apples - 5 **soggy** (adj.): unpleasantly wet and soft - 6 **to evolve** (v.): to develop by gradually changing - 7 **mist** (n.): light fog - 9 **squirrel** (n.): small animal with a long furry tail that climbs trees and eats nuts - 11 **to fend off** (v.): to defend o.s. - 12 **status** (n.). /-eɪ-/ social rank or position - 13 **to peer** (v.): to look very carefully or hard - 15 **moustache** (n.): /mə'stɑːʃ/ hair that grows on a man's upper lip - 16 **plus fours** (n. pl.): trousers with loose wide legs that are fastened just below the knee, worn by men esp. in the 1920s when playing golf - 21 **interloper** (n.): s.o. who enters a place or group where they should not be - 24 **scared** (adj.): frightened - 25 **solitary** (adj.): existing alone - 28 **coward** (n.): /'kaʊəd/ s.o. who is not at all brave - 28 **to improve** (v.): become better - 31 **pinafore** (n.): /'- - -/ a loose piece of clothing without sleeves worn over clothes to keep them clean (Schürze) - 34 **sanctity** (n.): (fml.) holy or religious character of a place - 35 **eager** (adj.): very excited about s.th. - 37 **clickie** (n.): (sl.) s.o. who is good at picking locks - 37 **WEST RIDING**: county of West Yorkshire (in the north of England) - 39 **to display** (v.): to show clearly - 43 **spacious** (adj.): large and having plenty of space - 45 **dresser** (n.): large piece of furniture with open shelves for storing plates etc. - 45 **plaster** (n.): substance consisting of lime (Kalk), water and sand (Gips)

- 52 **to varnish** (v.): to cover s.th. with a clear liquid, esp. things made of wood, to give them a shiny surface - 53 **tile** (n.): flat square piece of baked clay, used for covering floors - 53 **ivory** (n.): yellowish white colour - 54 **plinth** (n.): square block, usu. made of stone, that is used as a base for a statue - 57 **poised** (adj.): not moving but ready to move at any moment - 66 **bunched** (adj.): standing close together in a group - 71 **keen** (adj.): (here) very interested - 76 **lapse** (n.): failure to do s.th. you should do - 81 **to crouch** (v.): to lower your body close to the ground by bending your knees completely - 81 **orchard** (n.): place where fruit trees are grown - 84 **exasperation** (n.): state of being highly annoyed - 89 **presumably** (adv.): used to say that you think s.th. is likely to be true - 90 **to occur** (v.): /ə'kɜː/ (fml.) to happen - 102 **michaelmas daisy** (n.): kind of flower, late garden aster - 103 **gnarled** (adj.): /nɑːld/ rough and twisted with hard lumps - 110 **damson** (n.): kind of fruit (plum) - 114 **to squint** (v.): to look at s.th. with your eyes partly closed in order to see better - 116 **inkling** (n.): slight idea about s.th. - 120 **to relieve** (v.): to replace s.o. - 124 **sleuth** (n.): /uː/ (humor.) detective - 133 **to scowl** (v.): to look at s.o. in an angry way - 133 **disgust** (n.): very strong feeling of dislike that almost makes you sick - 141 **witch** (n.): woman who is supposed to have magic powers - 141 **wand** (n.): thin stick you hold in your hand to do magic tricks - 146 **windfall** (n.): piece of fruit that has fallen off a tree - 167 **insolent** (adj.): rude and not showing any respect - 167 **hesitant** (adj.): /'– – –/ uncertain abut what to do or say - 170 **sulky** (adj.): angry and silent - 175 **sultry** (adj.): (of a woman) attractive in a way that suggests a passionate nature - 175 **velvet** (n.): cloth with a soft surface on one side, used for making clothes (Samt) - 176 **vivacious** (adj.): /vɪ'veɪʃəs/ having a lot of energy and a happy attractive manner - 177 **to cuddle** (v.): to hold s.o. very close to you with your arms around them - 188 **SWAN LAKE**: ballet music by Peter Tchaikovsky, Russian composer (1840-93) - 190 **enthralled** (adj.): so interested that you pay a lot of attention to what you are seeing or hearing - 205 **tacit** (adj.): understood without being put into words - 206 **consent** (n.): /–'–/ permission to do s.th. - 207 **to wallop** (v.): (infml.) to hit s.o. very hard - 208 **to bewilder** (v.): to confuse s.o. - 208 **retribution** (n.): severe punishment - 209 **to cuss** (v.): (old-fashioned) to use rude words because you are annoyed by s.th. - 210 **irate** (adj.): /aɪ'reɪt/ extremely angry - 213 **to persist** (v.): to continue to do s.th. although it is difficult - 218 **to mope** (v.): to feel sorry for yourself - 220 **embarrassed** (adj.): /ɪm'bærəst/ ashamed, nervous or uncomfortable - 237 **evaporated milk**: milk which has been made thicker by removing some of the water (Kondensmilch) - 249 **to extract** (v.): /–'–/ to remove an object from somewhere - 274 **grateful** (adj.): feeling that you want to thank s.o. - 287 **GUY FAWKES**: /ˌgaɪ 'fɔːks/ November 5th, when in Britain people light fireworks and burn a guy on a bonfire. This is in memory of the time when Guy Fawkes tried to destroy Parliament in London in 1605. - 297 **to dwell upon** (v.): to think far too long about s.th. - 298 **ridicule** (n.): /'– – –/ unkind laughter or remarks intended to make s.o. seem stupid - 301 **wet** (adj.): (infml.) unable to make decisions - 303 **to dismiss** (v.): to refuse to consider any longer - 307 **conker** (n.): large shiny brown seed of the horse chestnut tree (Roßkastanie) - 321 **sexton** (n.): s.o. who takes care of a church building - 324 **hermit** (n.): s.o. who lives alone and has a simple way of life, usu. for religious reasons

Tasks

1: Brainstorming: did you play outside with other children when you were younger? What games did you play?

2: Establish the setting of the story by collecting all the details from the text. Take into consideration the children's language.

3: Examine the narrative perspective and its function. Discuss the interval between time of action and time of narration and its effect on the reader.

4: Find all the details that help you establish the group dynamics among the children. Consider the boys' and the girls' roles.

5: Compare the children's reaction to the man with that of the other village inhabitants. Can you give a plausible reason for his isolation in the village?

6: Examine the effect the dolls have on the children and try to find an explanation. What is the dolls' significance for the man?

7: Analyse the prejudices that are voiced against the man after his death. Try to find a psychologically convincing explanation.

8: Discuss the ending. What does it tell about the problems children may have with adults and what insight does it give into the first-person narrator?

9: Find examples of irony in the story that indicate that the first-person narrator is an adult.

RON BUTLIN

Ron Butlin lives and works in Edinburgh, Scotland. He has published two volumes of poetry as well as a collection of short stories.

The German Boy

The woman I can see standing outside in the pouring rain reminds me of Klaus, the German boy. It is the expression on her face: she looks... so desolate, so utterly unloved. People hurry past her as quickly as possible; if someone does smile, I watch her hesitate for a moment. Then she looks away.

When I came to the office about half-an-hour ago I passed her by pretending interest in a shop-display. From here, however, I can study her in perfect safety. Perhaps she is waiting for someone. I realize now that she could not have been taken in by my elaborate charade for it is repeated every few minutes by others - repeated too frequently to be convincing. At one time I might have pitied her, for that kind of cruelty comes easiest of all. Believe me, I know - Klaus taught me that.

This morning I have come to the office and done nothing. There is a pile of correspondence for me, some of it marked 'urgent'. Instead I stand and stare out of the window at the well-dressed woman opposite. She is in her mid-forties. I think she is crying but it is difficult to tell at this distance. She has glanced in my direction so I will move back from the window.

I remember my headmaster talking to us before Klaus was brought in.

'There is nothing special about him,' he said. 'Remember, he is just like the rest of us.'

When he came into the classroom for the first time, however, it was quite obvious he was not like the rest of us: Klaus looked different, he talked different and, even though he wore the same clothes as us, somehow he seemed to be dressed differently. Everyone looked at him and he looked at the floor. He had fair hair, very pale skin and was quite tall. His shoulders were trembling - an action his long arms increased proportionally, making his hands jerk as if they were receiving a series of small electric shocks.

'This is Klaus, he is going to join your class.' The headmaster was a small red-faced man who always looked as if he was too small and too red-faced to be comfortable. When he died a few months later from sunstroke I imagined him as having simply exploded one very hot afternoon.

My family talked a great deal about 'class' which for a long time I confused with my schoolfriends who were all of one class in both senses of the word. 'He is of a different class altogether' meant, to me, that someone was simply a few years older or younger than myself. And when my Aunt Claire happened to remark during an Open Day that Klaus was of a different class to the rest of the boys, I hastened to correct her saying that on the contrary he was the same age as myself and we sat next to each other and were the very best of friends. She said I was a very kind and thoughtful boy; and I replied excitedly that I was going to learn German. 'Of course you should help him to be at his ease, but you mustn't neglect your proper studies,' she concluded with a smile.

Klaus didn't even glance at the class he was about to join. He looked more uncomfortable than ever: his knees began shaking and his hands, in an effort to control the effects of the 'electric shocks', had grasped his jacket tightly at the sides - which served only to increase his nervous jerkings by the amount of 'give' in the material.

The headmaster ushered him to one side of a map of the world which had the British Empire coloured red, 'an unfortunate choice of colour' my aunt had observed during her visit. Then he indicated Germany and spoke to Klaus in German: he replied, '*Ja, mein Herr*' without raising his eyes from the floor. And then a moment later he did look up - not at the map, however, but at us; and he smiled, then blushed and returned his gaze to the floor. A boy sniggered. The headmaster plodded on.

'Klaus from Germany. This is Germany.' He indicated it again. '-*Deutschland*.' He smiled at Klaus then looked at us once more.

'*Deutschland* - that's "Germany" in German. Now, does anyone here speak German?' The boy who had sniggered before shouted out, '*Ja, mein Herr*' making us all laugh.

Klaus sat next to me. He didn't speak English but we managed somehow in Latin. He told me he had been born and brought up in Germany but when his father died his mother had married an Englishman. He had only been here a week but he liked it. He said that he and I were friends - *amici sumus*. That was nearly twenty years ago.

I really should get down to some work. Normally I work hard, very hard. In the name of Cochrane and Assocs., I deal in money: I buy it, sell it, lend it. I deal only with the certain people and in private. They have confidence in me. They assume that having maintained credibility in the past, then our house will do so in the future - and perhaps they are right, for as long as they trust us then we can do business and so justify that trust. In the course of time I am expected to become head of the firm. I would have liked that.

When I was a child our family was well-off. There was an inheritance which my father employed wisely. I attended public school before going up to Oxford to read Classics. I was hard-working rather than brilliant. My father died when I was in my third year and I returned home immediately, to be told that he had committed suicide. We were completely bankrupt. Everything had to be sold; I had to leave Oxford and begin working in the City. For the last ten years I have worked hard to restore the family name.

Last night we had a special dinner, Sylvia and I, to celebrate our wedding anniversary - we have been married for five years. Afterwards she said she was proud of me as a husband, lover and merchant banker. She kissed me.

Recently I have had occasion to go over our company books and it has become apparent to me that our business methods are as hopelessly out-of-date as our furniture and fittings; and with our present commitments it is too late to correct the situation. We will be finished by the end of the year. Strictly speaking we are finished already but as yet no one else knows. However, once word gets around the City, we will have to shut-up shop: for a company that is failing, especially an old company, may inspire pity - but never investment. I want to tell my wife. I want to tell my partners.

Instead I say nothing. I stand at my office window staring out into the street at a complete stranger standing in the pouring rain. She has hardly moved from where I first saw her. She must be soaked through and very cold now. She appears very unhappy - I would like to go over and speak to her, to say 'Don't worry' or something like that; or perhaps even to smile at her from here. I would like to, but I know I won't.

On his first night in our dormitory Klaus was given the bed next to mine and I could hear him crying. The room was in darkness but I could just make him out under the blankets. He was kneeling and bending forwards with his head pushing into the pillow.

'Klaus, Klaus,' I called in a low voice. Quietly I went over to him and sat on his bed.

"Don't cry, don't cry. You're here now. It will be good - you and me together. Honest.'

He made some reply in a voice muffled as much by his tears as by the blankets. He probably hadn't understood a word I had said. I sat with him for nearly half-an-hour while he cried, then I went back to bed. The next night was the same, and every night afterwards. During the day he was fine: he worked hard in class and joined in the games. Gradually his English improved. Each night, however, he cried himself to sleep. Then one day, during the morning break, he told me that from then on he was going to speak only in German - except to me, of course. At first I thought he was joking, but he wasn't.

The next class was arithmetic and near the end of the lesson our teacher began going over the problems out loud.

'Klaus, No. 4 please, the one about the reservoir.' Klaus stood up to give his answer. He seemed uncertain and he mumbled. The teacher asked him to repeat it. He spoke more clearly this time: '*Zwei Minuten.*' The class laughed and even the teacher joined in a little before asking him to repeat it in English.

'*Zwei Minuten.*" The class laughed even louder, but this time the teacher didn't even smile.

'In English, Klaus, if you please,' he said quite firmly.

'*Zwei Minuten,*' Klaus repeated; his fingers were gripping the sides of the desk-lid and his body shook. The teacher asked him again, and again the class went into uproar at his reply. His face was white. He was gripping the desk so tightly it rattled against the floor. He began repeating his answer: '*Zwei Minuten Zwei Minuten Zwei Minuten...*' He was staring ahead, quite oblivious to the noise about him.

The teacher didn't know what to do... He told Klaus to sit down and he wouldn't. To be quiet and he wouldn't. To stand in the corner and he wouldn't. '*Zwei Minuten Zwei Minuten...*' Tears were running down his cheeks and his voice was choking but he couldn't stop. Finally he was taken to the sick-room.

He came back afterwards but still refused to speak English. A few days later he was sent home. I have never seen him since and hardly even given him a moment's thought until now.

It has stopped raining. The woman is still waiting there but in the sunlight, she looks less miserable. She has been there for forty minutes now, at least.

To work. I suppose I have to fill up the day somehow and then return home. And I will have to think how to tell Sylvia that the business is collapsing.

She will have cooked dinner for my arrival tonight and we will eat together with the children. Afterwards I will read them a bedtime story, then we will probably watch TV. A few hours later it will be time to go to bed - and still I will not have told her.

And tomorrow I will return to the office; and the day after. There will be letters marked 'urgent', cables, meetings, luncheons, delicate negotiations and so forth. And every evening I will return home to Sylvia. Back and forwards; back and forwards I will go saying nothing.

The woman has turned to check her appearance in the shop-window. She is adjusting her hat. I watch as she crosses the road and now walks quickly past my window and down the street.

I have sat down in my executive leather chair. At any moment the telephone may ring or my secretary announce someone to see me - until then I will do nothing except rest my feet on the desk. For how long? I wonder.

'*Zwei Minuten Zwei Minuten...*' I hear Klaus say - which I now understand as meaning a lifetime, or as good as.

Annotations

3 **desolate** (adj.): /ˈdesələt/ feeling very sad and lonely - 4 **to hesitate** (v.): to pause before saying or doing s.th. - 9 **to be taken in** (v.): to be completely deceived - 9 **elaborate** (adj.): /ɪˈlæbərət/ carefully produced and full of details - 9 **charade** (n.): /ʃəˈrɑːd/ situation in which people pretend that s.th. is true and behave as if it were true, when everyone knows it is not really true - 15 **urgent** (adj.): very important and needing to be dealt with immediately - 29 **to tremble** (v.): to shake slightly in a way that you cannot control - 30 **to jerk** (v.): to move in short, sudden movements - 47 **to neglect** (v.): to pay too little attention to s.th. you should do - 49 **to glance** (v.): to look quickly at s.th. or s.o. - 51 **effort**

(n.): physical or mental energy - 52 **to increase** (v.): /-s/ to make s.th. larger in amount or degree - 54 **to usher** (v.): to help s.o. to get from one place to another - 60 **to blush** (v.): to become red in the face - 60 **to snigger** (v.): to laugh quietly, and often unkindly - 61 **to plod on** (v.): to keep working steadily - 74 **Assocs. = associates** (n.pl.): /'səʊʃiəts/ partners in work - 77 **credibility** (n.): quality of deserving to be believed and trusted - 79 **to justify** (v.): to be a good and acceptable reason for s.th. - 82 **inheritance** (n.): money or property that you receive from s.o. who has died - 83 **to read** (v.): (here) to study - 83 **Classics** (n. pl.): language, literature and history of Ancient Rome and Greece - 86 **suicide** (n.): /'suːɪsaɪd/ act of killing o.s. - 90 **anniversary** (n.): date on which s.th. special or important happened in a previous year - 96 **commitment** (n.): (here) amount of money that you have to pay regularly - 100 **to inspire** (v.): to make s.o. have a particular feeling - 109 **dormitory** (n.): /'---/ large room for several people to sleep in - 117 **muffled** (adj.): less loud and clear - 138 **uproar** (n.): /'--/ a lot of noise or angry protest about s.th. - 141 **oblivious** (adj.): /-'---/ not noticing s.th. that is going on around you - 145 **to choke** (v.): (of a voice) to sound strange and not very loud - 161 **cable** (n.): telegram - 162 **negotiations** (n. often pl.): official discussions between the representatives of two opposing groups - 167 **executive** (adj.): /-'---/ (here) expensive and of high quality

Tasks

1: Pre-reading: Try to imagine yourself in a foreign country and together with people whose language you neither understand nor speak. How would you feel? For a list of adjectives, consult a German-English dictionary (work with a partner.)

2: Define the narrative perspective and explain its function.

3: Collect all the information you can find about the first-person narrator and establish his social situation and his character. What would you do in his situation?

4: Analyse the treatment of time. Examine the function of the different time levels. What is the effect of the use of the present tense on the reader?

5: Watching the lonely woman in the street at the beginning, the narrator equates pity with "cruelty" (cf. line 12). Can you explain what he means?

6: The lonely woman in the street jogs the narrator's memory and he remembers his schooldays and the German boy Klaus. In two groups, collect all the information about the woman and Klaus. Write a character portrait of each one of them. What may they have in common?

7: What is meant by the narrator's Aunt Claire's remark that the fact that the British Empire is coloured red on a map is an "unfortunate choice of colour" (lines 55-6)?

8: Examine the linguistic misunderstanding between the narrator and his aunt about the word "class". What may be the aunt's underlying assumption?

9: Comment on Klaus's situation in the English school and try to explain why all of a sudden he refuses to speak English. Discuss in your group or with a partner if you find his behaviour psychologically convincing, and if yes, why.

10: Look at the end of the story. Why, do you think, does the narrator understand Klaus's "*zwei Minuten*" as a "lifetime"?

Acknowledgements

We are grateful to the following for permission to reproduce copyright material. Should we have failed to contact anyone in any particular instance, we would welcome enquiries.

Texts

© Wendy Wallace, "Karif" is taken from Kitty Fitzgerald (ed.), *Iron Woman. New Stories by Women*, published by Iron Press, North Shields, 1990 and reprinted by permission of the author.

Jane Gardam, "Swan" is taken from Jane Gardam *Showing the Flag*, published by Abacus, London, 1990 and reprinted by permission of David Higham Associates, London.

Elizabeth Raintree, "Sumac on a Sunday" is taken from Kitty Fitzgerald (ed.), *Iron Woman. New Stories by Women*, published by Iron Press, North Shields, 1990.

Jane Stone, "The Man" is taken from Esmore Jones (ed.) *British Short Stories of Today*, Penguin, Harmondsworth, 1987.

Ron Butlin "The German Boy" take from Esmore Jones (ed.), *British Short Stories of Today*, Penguin, Harmondsworth, 1987. (© Ron Butlin 1982).

Photographs

Donecker Foto, Karlsruhe: p. 29.
Bettina Lindenberg, München: pp. 47, 54.
Mauritius Bildagentur, Mittenwald: p. 36.
Qaizra Shahraz, Manchester: p. 12.